W9-CAY-845

A CALL TO
REVIVAL

A CALL TO
REVIVAL

Leo R. Van Dolson

REVIEW AND HERALD® PUBLISHING ASSOCIATION
HAGERSTOWN, MD 21740

Copyright © 1991 by
Review and Herald® Publishing Association

The author assumes full responsibility for the accuracy of all facts and quotations as cited in this book.

This book was
Edited by Richard W. Coffen
Designed by Bill Kirstein
Cover photos
    Main picture: T. Dietrich / H. Armstrong Roberts
    Inset: H. Abernathy / H. Armstrong Roberts
Typeset: 11.6/12 Zapf Book Light

Texts credited to NEB are from *The New English Bible*. © The Delegates of the Oxford University Press and the Syndics of the Cambridge University Press 1961, 1970. Reprinted by permission.

Texts credited to NIV are from the *Holy Bible, New International Version*. Copyright © 1973, 1978, International Bible Society. Used by permission of Zondervan Bible Publishers.

Bible texts credited to RSV are from the Revised Standard Version of the Bible, copyrighted 1946, 1952 © 1971, 1973.

Bible texts credited to TEV are from the *Good News Bible*—Old Testament: Copyright © American Bible Society 1976; New Testament: Copyright © American Bible Society 1966, 1971, 1976.

PRINTED IN U.S.A.

96 95 94 93 92 91   10 9 8 7 6 5 4 3 2 1

R&H Cataloging Service
Van Dolson, Leo R.
    Call to revival, A.

    1. Revivals 2. Spiritual life. 3. S.D.A.—Revival and reformation.
I. Title.
    269

ISBN 0-8280-0628-8

Contents

Preface

One basic theme ties the books of Joel, Micah, and Zephaniah together—the urgent need for revival and reformation in a time of spiritual and political crisis. Ancient Israel failed to fulfill its God-given role by responding to the messages of the prophets, accepting the Messiah, and evangelizing the world. Because they failed, the prophets' predictions of judgment and deliverance, which could have taken place if Israel had met the conditions, will find their final fulfillment in the end-time events foretold in the New Testament. Thus the study of these books is particularly appropriate as we consider our need of revival now.

Why did the prophets so universally focus on God's judgments? It was not to *scare*, but to *prepare*. God wanted Israel to know what their rebelliousness caused Him to do in order to save them. Likewise, He wants those living in the last fragment of time to be aware of the judgments He must send in order to fulfill completely the plan of salvation and restore the earth to what He originally intended it to be.

The immediate occasion of Joel's call to repentance was a locust plague that had devastated Palestine. This calamity foreshadowed the day of the Lord when both unfaithful Israelites and unresponsive pagans would receive retribution at the hands of the Lord's army. Because God allowed the locust plague and the subsequent attacks of unbelieving enemies, they are depicted as His servants for the punishment of the unfaithful. Both the locusts and the invading enemies of Israel foreshadow God's heavenly army, which will confront the rebellious powers of earth at the end of time and deliver His loyal people.

Joel's clear-ringing trumpet call challenges us to sense our need of individual repentance as the day of judgment draws near. Only as we respond to this call can we receive the "former" and "latter" rains that the Lord promises to pour upon His people.

The messages of the prophet Micah speak in a special way to those who have departed to some extent from His will and are in grave danger of being subject to His judgments. Micah was a younger contemporary of Isaiah, prophesying in the latter half of the eighth century B.C., during the reigns of three kings of Judah: Jotham (750-731 B.C), Ahaz (735-715 B.C.), and Hezekiah (729-686 B.C.). He ministered at a time when the kings and people of the northern 10 tribes of Israel were inviting the judgments of God by filling up the cup of their iniquity. The first appeal in Micah's book was to the people of the northern kingdom. But they failed to respond, and the Lord allowed them to be taken captive by the Assyrians in 722 B.C. God through Micah then concentrated on the people of Judah. In forceful, colorful language Micah inveighed against the wickedness of his countrymen. But he also offered hope to the repentant.

Zephaniah tells us that he prophesied "in the days of Josiah the son of Amon, king of Judah" (Zeph. 1:1). Josiah reigned from 639 to 609/608 B.C. Because Zephaniah predicted the fall of Nineveh (Zeph. 2:13), which occurred in 612 B.C., we might conclude that his prophetic ministry occupied the earlier years of Josiah's reign. It is possible that Zephaniah was a contemporary of Habakkuk and that he prophesied a few years before Jeremiah began his prophetic ministry in 626 B.C.

The burden of Zephaniah's short book is that, in view of the coming day of the Lord, Judah and the surrounding nations should repent and "seek righteousness" (Zeph. 2:3). He foresaw that the unfaithful in Judah and in neighboring nations would be destroyed or taken captive; only a faithful remnant of Israel would be left to inhabit their own land and that of their former enemies. This remnant of purified believers would see Jerusalem exalted to a position of leadership among the nations.

The remnant who survived the Babylonian captivity never did realize the fulfillment of God's promise to make Jerusalem the center of the nations. They and their offspring wandered progressively further from the covenant relationship with God. But God's purposes and promises will be fulfilled in principle to the remnant of God's last-day people, who finally will witness the establishment of the kingdom of Christ centered in the New Jerusalem in the earth made new.

CHAPTER

1

A Call to Revival

Knowing that time is short, Satan does everything that he can to keep God's people from responding to the call for reformation and revival that has sounded in the Adventist Church since its inception.

He disguises temptation and sin by dressing them alluringly. He hides greed and selfishness underneath the golden-threaded silk of materialistic well-being. He uses the soft green velvet of self-esteem to cover envy and jealousy. He cloaks lust and immorality in the scarlet satin of false love. He arranges the purple taffeta of supposedly justifiable indignation in such a way that it makes hate and anger appear acceptable. He clothes cowardly fear of what others will think in the sunny yellow chintz of self-deception. And Satan hides doubt and despair beneath the royal blue crepe of pseudo-intelligence.

But someday soon the fires of judgment will expose the cover-up. The holocaust of divine revelation will burn away the glamorous outer coverings that cloak favorite sins. Then nothing will be left but the charred remnants of blackened character.

It is because of Satan's ability to lead us into self-deception that the message God gives us through the writings of the prophet Joel is peppered with warnings of judgments to come. Under the direction of the Holy Spirit, the prophet sounded the warning trumpet of judgment in clear, ringing tones. Yet throughout his little book we find these warnings tempered with messages of hope for the erring. Along with the hope that his message brings, we discover a strong pastoral appeal for repentance.

A brief glance at the book of Joel reveals that it deals first with judgments to come (Joel 1:1-2:11). This is followed by a call to repentance (Joel 2:12-17), and finally by a section that outlines the results of true repentance (Joel 2:18-3:21).

Locusts Everywhere

Creeping, crawling, chewing locusts were everywhere that the prophet glanced in his vision—an overwhelming plague of insects. But were they really locusts? No. Joel understood that they represented a horde of strong, invincible invaders "whose teeth are [as] the teeth of a lion" (Joel 1:6).

It is entirely possible that there may have been a literal, unprecedented plague of locusts that devastated the southern kingdom of Israel in Joel's time. But the message that he received came couched in vivid prophetic symbolism designed to catch the attention and interest of those he addressed. His hearers could hardly have missed the unusual significance and timeliness of his startling message.

However, the Holy Spirit had another audience in mind. The hyperbole (purposeful exaggeration) that characterizes Joel's description of the army of locusts as well as other dramatic descriptions in his book indicates clearly that his writings contain last-day, judgment-hour significance. Of course, they were warnings from God to the people of his day. But they also were written for our admonition.

Notice four stages in the unprecedented locust plague described in verse 4—the palmerworms were followed by the locusts, which, in turn, were followed by cankerworms, and then caterpillars.

Pages 677 and 678 of the *SDA Bible Dictionary* describe the four words used in sequence in Joel 1:4 this way:

Gazam. "It is most probably the locust in the 1st stage of its development, hence wingless, though not a true larva such as a caterpillar. Some see in it the young adult."

'Arbeh. "It is thought that it is the African migratory locust . . . in its fully developed wing stage, in which it invades a country in swarms and deposits eggs. This locust is very common in Palestine."

Yeleq. "It is most probably the creeping, unwinged migratory locust in the last stage of development before it becomes a winged adult. Some have identified it with the newly hatched locust, which can jump but not crawl."

Chasîl. "The Dutch scientist F. Bruijel . . . sees it as the fully grown locust at the stage when it leaves Palestine."

Whatever the significance of these four stages, the emphasis seems to be on the completeness of the devastation that they cause. Locusts, locusts everywhere, sweeping over the fields, stripping the land of every last plant, and leaving drought, famine, and devastation. What a time of trouble! But aren't the locusts of materialism and selfishness plaguing the church today? Has the spiritual drought they have caused left us dusty, dry, and dead in the spiritual sense?

What Can We Do About It?

God particularly places the responsibility for the revival and reformation that is needed to overcome the spiritual deadness of His people on the shoulders of leaders and ministers (see Joel 1:13). Their responsibility involves sanctifying a fast, calling a solemn assembly, and gathering "the elders and all the inhabitants of the land into the house of the Lord" in order to "cry unto the Lord" (verse 14).

Appealing to the leaders of the church assembled at the 1973 Annual Council, then General Conference president Robert Pierson stated frankly, "A revival and reformation in our leadership and administration must come. Not until we let go of all these handfuls of earthly sand that we are clawing for and clinging to for dear life, and begin to cling to the Rock of Ages and seek His Spirit, can we ever hope to succeed in the assignment God has given His remnant church. Only as we seek the Holy Spirit as the source of power for our leadership, the energy for all our assignments, will we ever rise above the miserable limitations of our own abilities and break out into that glorious experience that God speaks of as the Loud Cry" (*Revival and Reformation*, pp. 16, 17).

His timely call to the leaders of the church at that time still speaks to us with the ring of desperate urgency. The burden is on the leaders to call the church to revival and reformation. But the church as a whole has a great responsibility in this matter too. It is up to every member to hear the call and to respond willingly and eagerly by calling on the Lord to bring the promised renewal.

The Day of the Lord

That the Holy Spirit speaks through Joel to those living in the last days is evident in the reference to the "day of the Lord" (verse 15) and the use of hyperbole, or purposeful exaggeration, in the descriptions of the extent of the judgments in chapter 1.

In chapter 2 Joel returns to his description of the day

of the Lord. Although the expression "the day of the Lord" can apply locally to the judgment of a city or nation, the primary sense seems to be an eschatological (last day) application to the second coming of Christ. New Testament writers understood the term that way (see 1 Thess. 5:2; 2 Peter 3:10).

In *The Great Controversy* Ellen White quotes the second chapter of Joel as a warning designed to arouse God's people from the Laodicean lethargy that characterizes the last-day church. She puts it as follows: "In view of that great day the word of God, in the most solemn and impressive language, calls upon His people to arouse from their spiritual lethargy and to seek His face with repentance and humiliation [Joel 2:1, 15-17, 12, 13, quoted] . . . .

"To prepare a people to stand in the day of God, a great work of reform was to be accomplished. God saw that many of His professed people were not building for eternity, and in His mercy He was about to send a message of warning to arouse them from their stupor and lead them to make ready for the coming of the Lord" (p. 311).

The alarm trumpet has been blowing in Zion for some time now, challenging us to prepare for the coming of the Lord, which is more "nigh at hand" (Joel 2:1) today than ever before. "Revival now" must be our constant response to God's challenge. Now, while we have an opportunity to submit ourselves to the working of the Holy Spirit, who alone can prepare us for a place in the eternal kingdom that will be established soon.

Have you thought recently about how wonderful it will be in heaven? Our modern prophet bears out the exquisite desirability of that place while at the same time pointing out the cost to the individual: "If Christ be in us the hope of glory, we shall walk even as He walked; we shall imitate His life of sacrifice to bless others; we shall drink of the cup, and be baptized with the baptism; we shall welcome a life of devotion, trial, and self-denial, for Christ's sake. Heaven will be cheap enough whatever sacrifice we may make to obtain it" (*Testimonies*, vol. 2, p. 73).

What about heaven appeals most strongly to you aside from the thought of seeing and talking with Jesus? Do you long for all tears to be wiped away? Are there certain Bible people you long to meet? Are there loved ones with whom you want to be united forever?

After describing how wonderful heaven will be in a series of *Review* articles, one of the early editors, Uriah Smith, closed with an appeal for commitment—an elevenfold "we must" commitment—that presents a challenge to all of us:

"We MUST be there.

"We MUST bask in the forgiving smiles of the God to whom we have become reconciled, and sin no more.

"We MUST have access to that exhaustless fount of vitality, the fruit of the tree of life, and never die.

"We MUST repose under the shadow of its leaves, which are for the service of the nations, and never again grow weary.

"We MUST drink from the life-giving fountain, and thirst nevermore.

"We MUST bathe in its silvery spray, and be refreshed.

"We MUST walk on its golden sands, and feel that we are no longer exiles.

"We MUST exchange the cross for the crown, and feel that the days of our humiliation are ended.

"We MUST lay down the staff and take the palm branch, and feel that the journey is done.

"We MUST put off the rent garments of our warfare, for the white robes of triumph, and feel that the conflict is ended and the victory gained.

"We MUST exchange the toil-worn, dusty girdle of our pilgrimage, for the glorious vesture of immortality, and feel that sin and the curse can nevermore pollute us" (July 21, 1874, p. 44; format adapted).

We *must* be there—and by God's grace we will be there. But in order to be there we must heed the warning trumpet call now. If we are to be ready when the last great trump announces the return of Christ, we must listen as its tones call us to final revival and reformation.

Locusts Again

Joel 2:3-11 compares the locust plague the prophet had previously described to a well-disciplined army that nothing can stop. This irresistible horde symbolizes the army of the Lord that will accompany Christ at His second coming and will participate in the harvest of the earth (see Matt. 24:30, 31; Rev. 19:11-14).

The description in Joel 2:10 applies only in a limited way to what a horde of locusts could do. The insects certainly could not cause earthquakes or shake the heavens. Something else must be responsible for such phenomena. Notice how the following descriptions of events surrounding the second coming of Christ in *The Great Controversy* fit Joel's depiction in verse 10 of what takes place on the day of the Lord:

"The earth shall quake." "The whole earth heaves and swells like the waves of the sea. Its surface is breaking up. Its very foundations seem to be giving way. Mountain chains are sinking. Inhabited islands disappear" (p. 637).

"The heavens shall tremble." "In the midst of the angry heavens is one clear space of indescribable glory, whence comes the voice of God like the sound of many waters, saying: 'It is done.' . . . That voice shakes the heavens and the earth" (p. 636).

"The sun and the moon shall be dark, and the stars shall withdraw their shining." "A dense blackness, deeper than the darkness of the night, falls upon the earth. . . . It is at midnight that God manifests His power for the deliverance of His people. The sun appears, shining in its strength. Signs and wonders follow in quick succession. . . . Dark, heavy clouds come up and clash against each other. The sun now and then breaks through, appearing like the avenging eye of Jehovah. Through a rift in the clouds there beams a star whose brilliancy is increased fourfold in contrast with the darkness. It speaks hope and joy to the faithful, but severity and wrath to the transgressors of God's law. . . . While these words of holy trust ascend to God [Ps. 46:1-3], the clouds sweep back, and the starry heavens are seen, unspeakably glorious in contrast with the black and angry firmament on either side" (pp. 636-639).

The Crucial Question

The appeal God later made in Zephaniah 2:3 appropriately challenges those of us who now face the imminent day of the Lord. We will study this in some detail in chapter 11. But because it contains a special promise of protection "in the day of the Lord's anger" it seems appropriate to introduce this verse here. "Seek ye the Lord, all ye meek of the earth, which have wrought his judgment; seek righteousness, seek meekness: it may be ye shall be hid in the day of the Lord's anger."

The expression of hope that "it may be ye shall be hid" takes on a much more certain note in a statement made in *Early Writings*: "I saw that Satan was at work . . . to distract, deceive, and draw away God's people, just now in this sealing time. I saw some who were not standing stiffly for present truth. Their knees were trembling, and their feet sliding, because they were not firmly planted on the truth, and the covering of Almighty God could not be drawn over them while they were thus trembling.

"Satan was trying his every art to hold them where they were, until the sealing was past, until the covering was drawn over God's people, and they left without a shelter from the burning wrath of God, in the seven last plagues. God has begun to draw this covering over His people, and it will soon be drawn over all who are to have a shelter in the day of slaughter" (p. 44).

Apparently, Satan does not concentrate so intently on persuading Adventists to give up their faith entirely (although he enjoys doing that) as he does on merely holding us where we are—in a state of Laodicean apathy—until it is too late for us to do anything about it. We cannot let him get away with that trick. Now, while the final warning trumpet is sounding; now, as we face the imminent day of the Lord; now, when God is drawing His protecting cover over those who will be hidden from harm during the great time of trouble; NOW, by God's help, we must meet the challenge of our greatest and most urgent need—a revival of true godliness among us.

CHAPTER

2

The Great Churchquake

Dramatically and appealingly Joel calls God's people to repentance, revival, and reformation. The word *therefore* that begins verse 12 of chapter 2 refers to the previous section, which deals with alarms and warnings of judgment to come. In this part of the book of Joel we discover that the trumpet call of reformation follows the trumpet call to revival. There can be no true revival without subsequent reformation.

On October 17, 1989, an earthquake that measured 7.1 on the Richter scale rocked the San Francisco Bay Area, causing much damage and the loss of nearly 100 lives. Most of these fatalities occurred in the collapse of the upper deck of the Nimitz Freeway in Oakland.

October 17 was "Fall Picnic Day" at Pacific Union College, my alma mater. Where did the students choose to go for their fall outing? Golden Gate Park in San Francisco! Although the picnic-goers had scattered by 5:04 p.m., when the earthquake struck, most still were in the Bay Area. One of the students was traveling eastward on the Bay Bridge's lower deck when the upper deck collapsed. "It looked like a garage door closing," reported the student, who was only a few seconds from being at that spot.[1]

Another group of students had gone to the Lick Observatory in San Jose. On the return trip they had to choose which freeway they would take, Interstate 880 through Oakland or Interstate 680, which runs through Walnut Creek to the east. They chose I-680. Had they chosen I-880, they would have been traveling along the Nimitz Freeway at the time the earthquake caused the freeway's top level to crash down on the lower level.

That section of the approach to the Bay Bridge was built before designers had opportunity to learn from later earthquakes that arranging reinforcing steel in horizontal circles around the vertical strands placed in the concrete pillars that supported the upper decks would have prevented their collapse. It can be expected, now that this technique has been learned, that if upper decks are allowed to be added to future freeways, this technique will be required to prevent such collapses. Reports coming from San Francisco indicated that the high rises that were built using techniques developed from lessons learned during previous earthquakes withstood the heavy shocks quite successfully.

Revelation 16:18-20 predicts an earthquake that will be of such magnitude that every island and mountain will be moved out of place. Ellen White gives us this vivid description: "The mountains shake like a reed in the wind, and ragged rocks are scattered on every side. There is a roar as of a coming tempest. The sea is lashed into fury. There is heard the shriek of a hurricane like the voice of demons upon a mission of destruction. The whole earth heaves and swells like the waves of the sea. Its surface is breaking up. Its very foundations seem to be giving way. Mountain chains are sinking. Inhabited islands disappear. The seaports that have become like Sodom for wickedness are swallowed up by the angry waters. . . . The proudest cities of the earth are laid low" (*The Great Controversy*, p. 637).

Not even "earthquake-proof" buildings will be able to stand in the final great upheaval. Will we be among God's earthquake-proof people? The decision is ours. We can learn important lessons from those who have failed to prepare for God's judgments in the past. We Adventists should be acutely aware that the final judgment is just ahead.

Unprecedented Intensity

A sudden whirlwind of startling events broke out in Eastern Europe in 1989. The Berlin Wall was torn down and Russian troops and arms were removed from places that they had occupied since World War II. Some form of democratic government quickly replaced the single-party system that long dominated in those countries. People in the West who had assumed that the status quo in that part of Europe was bound to last a long time were startled by such sudden changes. Adventists were reminded that Ellen White had written long ago that "the final movements will be rapid ones" (*Testimonies*, vol. 9, p. 11).

The unprecedented intensity in the increase of the traditional signs of Christ's return leads many today to realize that it will not be long before the little cloud, about half the size of a man's hand, heralds the great day when Jesus will come.

One example of the increase of these portents is the number of major earthquakes that have been reported:[2]

Sixth century = 1
Ninth century = 1
Eleventh century = 1
Thirteenth century = 3
Sixteenth century = 2
Seventeenth century = 2

Eighteenth century = 7 (including the great Lisbon earthquake)

Nineteenth century = 10

Twentieth century = 88

Yet Jesus predicted that these signs of the times would be neither the most significant nor the ultimate ones (see Matt. 24:8).

The most consequential and truly ultimate signs focus on the *church* rather than the world. We often apply the words of Matthew 24:12, "Because iniquity shall abound, the love of many shall wax cold," to the world. But careful study of verses 9 to 11 reveal a startling fact: Jesus is talking about the *church*. His words must apply to the remnant church in particular. This application is borne out in verse 14, which indicates the fulfillment of the special mission delegated to those who are given the responsibility of proclaiming the three angels' messages. This verse is the ultimate sign. When the gospel is "preached in all the world for a witness unto all nations," Jesus says, "then shall the end come."

What Christ predicted about the condition of the remnant church in verse 12 *is* taking place. Among those commissioned to warn the world of Jesus' soon coming, the love of many *has* waxed cold. We do not have to document the gruesome details. They are visible even to the casual onlooker.

Yet in the midst of the frigid unresponsiveness of many of God's people will be seen the blazing fire of the latter rain. It will spread "like fire in the stubble" (Ellen White, in *Review and Herald*, Dec. 15, 1885). "Light will be communicated to *every* city and town" (*Evangelism*, p. 694).

The Call to Revival and Reformation

Without doubt, one of the most significant happenings in our church today is the call to revival and reformation now being sounded throughout the Adventist world. My wife and I were invited to the Far Eastern Division in November of 1989 to join a team of workers from the United States who spent a month covering the entire division with the challenge to revival and reformation. That call is sounding throughout the Adventist world.

A familiar appeal written by Ellen White that first appeared in the *Review* on March 22, 1887—more than 100 years ago—is now receiving well-deserved attention. Its setting was the revival that had taken place at Battle Creek College and the events that followed. In her appeal she stated that a genuine revival is "the greatest and most urgent of all our needs."

Immediately following that statement, Ellen White pointed out what our part is to be in such a revival: "There must be earnest effort to obtain the blessing of the Lord, not because God is not willing to bestow His blessing upon us, but because we are unprepared to receive it. Our heavenly Father is more willing to give His Holy Spirit to them that ask Him, than are earthly parents to give good gifts to their children. But it is *our work*, by *confession*, *humiliation*, *repentance*, and *earnest prayer*, to fulfill the conditions upon which God has promised to grant us His blessing" (*Selected Messages*, book 1, p. 121, italics supplied).

"Conditions," "earnest effort," "our work"—some prefer to avoid these terms. But there they are. If we are to have a revival of true godliness that will supply our most urgent need, we *must* meet the conditions. How? Let us analyze the four actions that God through His messenger tells us will help bring about revival.

1. Confession—Proverbs 28:13 warns that "he that covereth his sins shall not prosper," then adds "but whoso confesseth and forsaketh them shall have mercy." By God's grace "we must work to take the stumbling blocks out of the way. We must remove every obstacle. Let us confess and forsake every sin, that the way of the Lord may be prepared" (*ibid.*, p. 123).

Can this really happen? It must if we are to have a genuine revival in our church. But it cannot be accomplished by church decree. It will involve an individual experience of heartfelt confession on the part of each of us.

Ellen White's description of what "might have been" shows us what can be if we learn from this experience. In a letter to the Battle Creek church dated January 5, 1903, she wrote: "One day at noon I was writing of the work that might have been done at the last General Conference if the men in positions of trust had followed the will and way of God. . . . [Then] I seemed to be witnessing a scene in Battle Creek. We were assembled in the auditorium of the Tabernacle. . . . The meeting was marked by the presence of the Holy Spirit. The work went deep, and some present were weeping aloud.

"One arose from his bowed position and said that in the past he had not been in union with certain ones and had felt no love for them, but that now he saw himself as he was. . . . The speaker turned to those who had been praying, and said: 'We have something to do. We must confess our sins, and humble our hearts before God.' He made heartbroken confessions and then stepped up to several of the brethren, one after another, and extended his hand, seeking forgiveness. Those to whom he spoke sprang to their feet, making confession and asking forgiveness, and they fell upon one another's necks, weeping. The spirit of confession spread through the entire congregation. . . .

"There was rejoicing such as never before had been heard in the Tabernacle.

"Then I aroused from my unconsciousness, and for

a while could not think where I was. My pen was still in my hand. The words were spoken to me: '*This might have been.* All this the Lord was waiting to do for His people. All heaven was waiting to be gracious.' I thought of where we might have been had thorough work been done at the last General Conference, and an agony of disappointment came over me as I realized that what I had witnessed was not a reality" (*Testimonies*, vol. 8, pp. 104-106).

Someday soon it must become a reality.

2. *Humiliation*—When someone asked Francis of Assisi why he was so influential and seemed to have so much power to touch people's hearts and lives, he replied, "Well, I've been thinking about that myself lately, and this is why: The Lord looked down from heaven upon the earth and said, 'Where can I find the weakest, the littlest, the meanest man on the face of the earth?' Then He saw me and said, 'I've found him! Now I'll work through him. He won't be proud of it. He'll see that I am only using him because of his littleness and insignificance.' "

This is the kind of humble submission to the will of God that must characterize us today. "The church must arouse to action. The Spirit of God can never come in until she prepares the way. There should be earnest searching of heart. . . . There should be, not a clothing of the body with sackcloth, as in ancient times, but a deep humiliation of soul" (*Selected Messages*, book 1, p. 126).

When we are willing to humble ourselves, to empty ourselves in order to be willing vessels to hold the mercies of God, the Lord will be able to use us.

3. *Repentance*—As indicated above, revival has to be an individual work. Church committees cannot legislate it. All of us need to search our own hearts and repent of the sins revealed. Ellen White spells this out in specific detail: "We must enter upon the work individually. We

must pray more, and talk less." "We must seek the Lord with true penitence; we must with deep contrition of soul confess our sins, that they may be blotted out" (*ibid.*, pp. 122, 125).

The classic definition of repentance is "a godly sorrow for and a turning from sin." What is the import of the earnest plea of Joel 2:12 in which God directs His people to "turn ye even to me with all your heart"? A more accurate translation of *turn* might be "turn back" or "return."

God calls for genuine heart repentance—repentance that is characterized, according to Joel 2:12, by fasting, weeping, and mourning. Repentance is to be accompanied by outward acts of devotion and penitence. But it must come from the heart. Joel 2:13 admonishes, "Rend your heart, and not your garments, and turn unto the Lord your God."

The following Ellen White quotations indicate to us how far our turning from sin must go. "I saw that many were neglecting the preparation so needful and were looking to the time of 'refreshing' and the 'latter rain' to fit them to stand in the day of the Lord and to live in His sight. . . . I saw that none could share the 'refreshing' unless they obtain the victory over every besetment, over pride, selfishness, love of the world, and over every wrong word and action" (*Early Writings*, p. 71).

Ellen White states: "The refreshing or power of God comes only on those who have prepared themselves for it by doing the work which God bids them, namely, cleansing themselves from all filthiness of the flesh and spirit, perfecting holiness in the fear of God" (*Testimonies*, vol. 1, p. 619).

This challenge is not just earthshaking, it is churchquaking! We live in the time of the final churchquake. Ellen White refers to it as the "shaking time."

"I asked the meaning of the shaking I had seen and

was shown that it would be caused by the straight testimony called forth by the counsel of the True Witness to the Laodiceans. . . . Some will not bear this straight testimony. They will rise up against it, and this is what will cause a shaking among God's people. . . . This testimony must work deep repentance; all who truly receive it will obey it and be purified. . . . [Remember, we are discussing repentance. She refers to it as "deep."]

"Said the angel, 'Look ye!' My attention was then turned to the company I had seen who were mightily shaken. I was shown those whom I had before seen weeping and praying in agony of spirit. The company of guardian angels around them had been doubled and they were clothed with an armor from their head to their feet. . . . They had obtained the victory. . . .

"I heard those clothed with the armor speak forth the truth with great power. It had effect. . . . I asked what had made the great change. An angel answered, 'It is the latter rain, the refreshing from the presence of the Lord, the loud cry of the third angel'" (*Early Writings*, pp. 270, 271).

Notice how clear it is that the shaking that leads some to deep repentance, to victory, and to being clothed with Christ's armor from head to feet *must take place before* the latter rain and loud cry. This work of repentance is much broader and deeper than anything we have experienced up until this time.

4. Earnest Prayer—At the center of the revival experience is earnest, Spirit-led prayer. This kind of prayer, entered into by the disciples before the initial Pentecost experience, is instructive.

"The disciples prayed with intense earnestness. . . . [They] felt their spiritual need and cried to the Lord for the holy unction that was to fit them for the work of soul saving. They did not ask for a blessing for themselves merely. They were weighted with the burden of the salvation of souls. They realized that the gospel was to be carried to the world, and they claimed the power that Christ had promised" (*The Acts of the Apostles*, p. 37).

It is this kind of prayer that is involved in rending our hearts instead of our garments. Such prayer will indeed be churchquaking.

What was the result of such earnest praying in the days of the apostles? "The Spirit came upon the waiting, praying disciples with a fullness that reached every heart. The Infinite One revealed Himself in power to His church. It was as if for ages this influence had been held in restraint, and now Heaven rejoiced in being able to pour out upon the church the riches of the Spirit's grace" (*ibid.*, p. 38).

"So It May Be Now"

Speaking of the outpouring of the Holy Spirit at Pentecost, Ellen White declares, "*So it may be now*. Let Christians put away all dissension and give themselves to God for the saving of the lost. Let them ask in faith for the promised blessing, and it will come" (*Testimonies*, vol. 8, p. 21).

Where do we begin? Joel 2:15-17 indicates the place: "Blow the trumpet in *Zion*, sanctify a fast, call a solemn assembly; gather the people, sanctify the congregation, assemble the elders, gather the children, and those that suck the breasts: let the bridegroom go forth of his chamber, and the bride out of her closet. Let the priests, the ministers of the Lord, weep between the porch and the altar, and let them say, Spare thy people, O Lord, and give not thine heritage to reproach." The call is to everyone in the church.

The two trumpets of Joel 2 represent the call to *revival* (Joel 2:1) and the call to *reformation* (verse 15).

The loud ringing blast of these trumpets urges us now to awaken from our Laodicean sleeping sickness and to make sure that we have our priorities straight. Someday soon the church will respond so fully to this call that the greatest display of the love of Christ will be seen in our world. This work of revival and reformation will not cease until Jesus comes. Such an experience is our greatest need. It *must* come soon. It *will* take place soon. If so, Why not now? Why not with us? Why not?

---

[1] Pacific Union College *Viewpoint*, Winter, 1989, p. 1.

[2] Data compiled from *Encyclopedia Americana, World Book Encyclopedia,* and *The World Almanac and Book of Facts.*

C H A P T E R

3

Springtime
and Harvest

Joel predicted that God's repentant people will rejoice in the restoration of the seasons of rain in the Holy Land (see Joel 2:18-27). Under inspiration he went on to foretell that there would be two special outpourings of the Holy Spirit on God's people when they were prepared for them, which are prefigured in "the former rain" and "the latter rain" (verse 23).

"The ruling feature of the Palestinian climate is the division of the year into a rainy and a dry season. Towards the end of October heavy rains begin to fall for a day or several days at a time. This is what the Bible calls the *early* or *former* rain, literally the *Pourer*. It opens the agricultural year; the soil, hard and cracked by the long summer, is loosened and the farmer begins ploughing. Till the end of November the rainfall is not large, but increases from December to February, abates in March, and is practically over by the middle of April. The *latter rains* of Scripture are the heavy showers of March and April" (Smith's *Geography of the Holy Land*, pp. 62, 63).

The early rains came at the time of the autumnal equinox in the Holy Land. But the rain continued through the winter. The latter rains fell at the vernal equinox in the spring. The King James Version of Joel 2:23 speaks of the early or former rain coming "moderately" as compared with the latter rain. In his Pentecost sermon, Peter referred to the outpouring of the Holy Spirit as a fulfillment of Joel's prophecy (see Acts 2:16-21). But it only partially fulfilled the prediction.

The Harvest

The latter rain, coming in the spring, prepared the grain for the harvest. In the early part of April barley was harvested, and soon after, the wheat was gathered in. The harvests took place earlier in the lowlands but were completed by the end of June in the uplands. The fact that in the Holy Land springtime was followed by harvest teaches us something about the final harvest.

In Matthew 13:39 Jesus tells us that "the harvest is the end of the world." Now is earth's springtime. It is time for the latter rain and the latter rain will be followed by the harvest—the great final harvest that takes place at the end of time. Verses 12-14 of Joel 3 indicate that one aspect of the harvest that comes as a result of the latter rain is that it includes the judgment of the nations.

The final harvest of souls is far beyond feeble human resources. We need to receive the promised "latter rain" of God's Spirit poured out on us in Pentecostal blessing and power if we are ever to prepare the world for the coming of Jesus. We are told that "the whole heavenly treasure awaits our demand and reception. . . . This is the work that the Lord would have every soul prepared to do at this time" (*Testimonies to Ministers*, p. 510).

Ever since Pentecost in A.D. 31—the year that Christ died—the power of the Holy Spirit has been at work in the church. The early rain, which began at that Pentecost, has been continuously available to God's people.

For this reason the words that Jesus addressed to the disciples while sitting by the side of Jacob's well in Sychar are most appropriate for His disciples today. "He looked over the fields of grain that were spread out before Him, their tender green touched by the golden sunlight" (*The Desire of Ages*, p. 191).

As Jesus pointed His disciples to the scene, He instructed, "Say not ye, There are yet four months, and then cometh harvest? behold, I say unto you, Lift up your eyes, and look on the fields; for they are white already to harvest" (John 4:35).

As Christ spoke He looked on the group of people that the Samaritan woman was leading to the well. It was four months to the time for harvesting grain, but here was a harvest ready to be gathered in.

The Challenge of the Harvest

Our current success in soul winning could make us satisfied with the progress of our work. But it should not. However, it does help us recognize that today the world field *is* "white to the harvest." Certainly the great harvesttime cannot be far away. A special challenge comes to us from Proverbs 10:5: "He that sleepeth in harvest is a son that causeth shame."

The approaching harvest of the earth demands that we as a church awake from our Laodicean lethargy and direct our energies to reaching every region and every ethnic, cultural, and social group. According to Revelation 14:6, a vast multitude waits to be gathered from "every nation, and kindred, and tongue, and people."

While attending a bidivision council in Rio de Janeiro a few years ago, I picked up a motto that nicely pinpoints the soul-winning spirit in Latin America:

"From country to country until we have reached every country.

"From island to island until we have reached every island.

"From city to city until we have reached every city.

"From town to town until we have reached every town.

"From village to village until we have reached every village.

"From house to house until we have reached every house.

"From person to person until we have reached every person."

It is my conviction that Adventists everywhere should adopt this motto. But we need to keep in mind that the final harvest of souls is far beyond our feeble human resources. We need the promised outpouring of the "latter rain" of God's Spirit in Pentecostal blessing and power to prepare the world for the coming of Jesus. It is harvesttime. But "where are the reapers to garner in The sheaves of the good from the fields of sin"?

"The Holy Spirit is waiting for channels through whom to work. . . . The Spirit of God will be poured out upon the church just as soon as the vessels are prepared to receive it" (*"That I May Know Him,"* p. 330).

Power Now

Actually, we should not sit back waiting and longing for the future outpouring of the latter rain. We cannot expect the latter rain until we have taken full advantage of the blessing of the early rain. We have the promise—"The descent of the Holy Spirit upon the church is looked forward to as in the future; but it is the privilege of the church to have it now. Seek for it, pray for it, believe for it. We must have it, and Heaven is waiting to bestow it" (*Evangelism*, p. 701).

The power Christ promised to give His church through the Holy Spirit is ours *now*. But the full and final manifestation of the Spirit's presence and power in the church will be revealed in the latter rain.

What a glorious future is predicted when we become so intensely earnest about our need of the Holy Spirit that we follow the example of the disciples in the preparations they made immediately prior to Pentecost to receive the outpouring of the Spirit.

What followed that outpouring? "The sword of the Spirit, newly edged with power and bathed in the lightnings of heaven, cut its way through unbelief. Thousands were converted in a day" (*The Acts of the Apostles*, p. 38).

The counsel is given us: "The promise of the Spirit is a matter little thought of. . . . Minor matters occupy the attention, and the divine power which is necessary for the growth and prosperity of the church, and which would bring all other blessings in its train, is lacking though offered in its infinite plentitude" (*Testimonies*, vol. 8, p. 21).

What Are We Waiting For?

When the outpouring of the Holy Spirit in the latter rain takes place, the world will quickly realize that the Lord is "in the midst of Israel" (Joel 2:27). The character and goodness of Christ will be manifested in His people and the honest of heart will be attracted to the church.

Notice the specific kinds of people Joel indicates will be included in the reception of the final great outpouring of the Holy Spirit—"all flesh," "your sons and your daughters," "old men," "young men," "servants," and "handmaids" (verses 28, 29). In other words, no one who has made the proper preparation will be excluded.

With God anxiously waiting to grant all of us this greatly needed outpouring, what are we waiting for? Why do we not make this our first priority?

Even Satan is worried that we will begin to take the

promise of the latter rain seriously and start doing something about it. "There is nothing that Satan fears so much as that the people of God shall clear the way by removing every hindrance so that the Lord can pour out His Spirit upon a languishing church and an impenitent congregation. If Satan had his way, there would never be another awakening, great or small, to the end of time. . . . Wicked men and devils cannot hinder the work of God or shut out His presence from the assemblies of His people, if they will, with subdued, contrite hearts, confess and put away their sins, and in faith claim His promises. Every temptation, every opposing influence, whether open or secret, may be successfully resisted, 'not by might, nor by power, but by my spirit, saith the Lord of hosts' (Zech. 4:6)" (*Selected Messages*, book 1, p. 124).

If Satan is worried even now, perhaps we should start giving him something to really be concerned about. The entire universe is waiting for us to take the work of preparation seriously and do our part in bringing about the latter rain.

When the Latter Rain Comes

The outpouring of the Holy Spirit in the latter rain will be given to God's people to finish His work on earth and to prepare the way for the second coming of Christ. The work of the gospel will be finished under the loud cry of Revelation 18:1-4 that results from the outpouring of the latter rain. "When divine power is combined with human effort, the work will spread like fire in the stubble. God will employ agencies whose origin man will be unable to discern; angels will do a work" (Ellen White, in *Review and Herald*, Dec. 15, 1885).

"The workers will be surprised by the simple means that He will use to bring about and perfect His work of righteousness" (*Testimonies to Ministers*, p. 300).

As the angel of Revelation 18 adds his voice to those of the three angels who preceded him, the "loud cry" will fill the earth. "Before the final visitation of God's judgments upon the earth, there will be among the people of the Lord such a revival of primitive godliness as has not been witnessed since apostolic times" (*The Great Controversy*, p. 464). "Servants of God, with their faces lighted up and shining with holy consecration, will hasten from place to place to proclaim the message from heaven. By thousands of voices, all over the earth, the warning will be given" (*ibid.*, p. 612).

"Light will be communicated to every city and town" (*Evangelism*, p. 694).

"In . . . Africa, in the Catholic lands of Europe and of South America, in China, in India, in the islands of the sea, and in all the dark corners of the earth, God has in reserve a firmament of chosen ones that will yet shine forth amidst the darkness, revealing clearly to an apostate world the transforming power of obedience to His law" (*ibid.*, pp. 706, 707).

"These conversions to truth will be made with a rapidity that will surprise the church, and God's name alone will be glorified" (*Selected Messages*, book 2, p. 16).

Eternal Spring Will Follow

Springtime leads to harvest. But earth's harvest will lead to eternal spring. The pessimist who penned the words "Spring is too rainy and summer too hot, fall is soon over but winter is not" is to have his underlying wish after all! Soon we will dwell in a land of eternal spring.

The final harvest will take place soon. Meeting the challenge of this crisis of opportunity takes *total commitment*. We are told, "Perilous times are before us. Everyone who has a knowledge of the truth should awake and place himself, body, soul, and spirit, under the discipline of God" (*Testimonies*, vol. 8, p. 298). Only such a commitment is worthy of this last, glorious hour of earth's history.

In a sermon to the General Conference session of 1889, Uriah Smith spoke on the history and the future work of Seventh-day Adventists. He described the work and trials facing the church. But he ended on a glorious note, describing how wonderful heaven will be: "I see there a land which stands out in wonderful contrast to this. . . . I see fields smiling in living green, trees majestic in their wealth of verdure, flowers dazzling with their rainbow hues, and on neither field nor tree nor flower do I see the touch of frost or the pale hand of decay. . . . I see every eye sparkling with the fullness of the joy that reigns within. I see on every cheek the bloom of eternal youth and everlasting health. I see every limb lithe and strong. I see the lame man leaping as an hart. I see the blind gazing with rapture on the celestial glory. I see the deaf listening enchanted to the heavenly melody. I see the dumb joining with loud voice in the anthems of praise. I see the mother clasping to her bosom the children she had lost awhile in the land of the enemy, but now recovered forever. I see long-parted friends meet in eternal reunion. I see a river so pure and clear, so charged with every element of refreshment, and life, that it is called 'the river of life.' I see a tree overarching all, so full of healing in its leaves, so vivifying in its fruits, that it is called 'the tree of life.' I see a great white throne in whose effulgence there is no need of moon or sun to give us light. I hear a voice saying to that victorious company, 'This is your rest forever; and you shall no more be acquainted with grief; for there shall be no more pain or death, and sorrow and mourning have forever fled away.' And in all the universe I then see no trace of sin or suffering, but I hear from every world and from every creature, a joyous anthem, like the sound of many waters, going up to God; and they say, Blessing, and honor, and glory, and power be unto Him that sitteth upon the throne and unto the lamb forever and ever.

"Such is the goodly land we may go up and possess. Such is the land that awaits every one of us who is faithful to the end" (*General Conference Bulletin*, Oct. 29, 1889, p. 107).

It's harvesttime! That is our special challenge today. But what gives us the courage and the commitment to do our part in preparing for the final harvest is the thrilling promise of the eternal spring that is sure to follow.

It will bring a permanent end to cancer, and to all disease. It will lead to us knowing ourselves even as we are known by God Himself. Human beings will then be able to travel without clumsy space vehicles or space suits to the farthest reaches of space in an extremely short span of time. Our travel through space will begin with a guided tour that will take us through the gloriously spectacular open space in Orion to the sea of glass and through the magnificently tall and shimmering gates of pearl into the City of God itself.

It's harvesttime! Let's go home.

4

The Valley of Decision

The last chapter in the truly significant book of Joel begins with a description of God's judgments on the nations in the valley of Jehoshaphat (meaning "Yahweh judges"). The last-day nature of this passage becomes apparent in verses 12 through 14: "Let the heathen be wakened, and come up to the valley of Jehoshaphat: for there will I sit to judge all the heathen round about. Put ye in the sickle, for the harvest is ripe: come, get you down; for the press is full, the fats overflow; for their wickedness is great. Multitudes, multitudes in the valley of decision: for the day of the Lord is near in the valley of decision."

Comparing these verses with Revelation 14:15-20 reveals many parallels between the two passages. The "sickle" is prominent in Revelation 14 as the "harvest of the earth is ripe." The grapes also "are fully ripe," paralleling Joel's statement that "the press is full, the fats overflow." These comparisons can be more dramatically and clearly seen when we view them in chart form:

Figures used	Joel 3:13	Rev. 14:15-20
Harvest	is ripe	of the earth is ripe
Winepress	press is full	grapes are fully ripe; winepress was trodden

Because there is no question but that Revelation 14 clearly portrays the final harvest at the end of the world, Joel 3:12-14 must also point to the final judgment. Apparently, John the revelator was quoting Joel indirectly when he penned these words.

How many of the nations of the earth are involved in the judgment pictured in Joel 3:1, 2? The New International Version translates verse 1 and the first part of verse 2 this way: "In those days and at that time, when I restore the fortunes of Judah and Jerusalem, I will gather all nations."

In order to understand this passage fully we need to keep in mind that "all nations" (verse 2), "all the men of war" (verse 9), including "the weak" (verse 10), and "all the heathen" (verse 12) are gathered in the valley of God's judgment (verse 12) or the valley of punishment (verse 14, Septuagint).

"Multitudes" are gathered in the valley of decision. Ellen White translates "multitudes" into "millions": "The day of the Lord is approaching with stealthy tread; but the supposed great and wise men know not the signs of Christ's coming or of the end of the world. Iniquity abounds, and the love of many has waxed cold.

"There are thousands upon thousands, millions upon millions, who are now making their decision for eternal life or eternal death. The man who is wholly absorbed in his counting room, the man who finds pleasure at the gaming table, the man who loves to indulge perverted appetite, the amusement lover, the frequenters of the theater and the ballroom, put eternity out of their reckoning. The whole burden of their life is, What shall we eat? what shall we drink? and wherewithal shall we be clothed? They are not in the procession that is moving heavenward. They are led by the great apostate, and with him will be destroyed.

"Unless we understand the importance of the moments that are swiftly passing into eternity, and make ready to stand in the great day of God, we shall be unfaithful stewards" (*Testimonies*, vol. 6, pp. 406, 407).

The Day of the Lord

In chapter 3 Joel reaches the climax toward which he has been building. In Joel 1:15 the prophet states that the destruction that will be brought by the Almighty is at hand. In chapter 2, verses 1 and 2 he adds that it will be a day of darkness and gloominess. In verse 31 of that chapter he mentions that signs in the heavens precede the day of the Lord. Finally in chapter 3:12-14 he comes to the full explanation that the expression "day of the Lord" particularly points to judgment and the harvest of the earth.

What two sides gather in the valley of decision for final battle? "Proclaim ye this among the Gentiles; Prepare war, wake up the mighty men, let all the men of war draw near; let them come up: Beat your plowshares into swords, and your pruninghooks into spears: let the weak say, I am strong. Assemble yourselves, and come, all ye heathen, and gather yourselves together round about: thither cause thy mighty ones to come down, O Lord" (Joel 3:9-11).

Here is the final Armageddon. Christ and His armies will confront the confederacy that Satan has gathered from this world in the last days.

Joel predicts that the time will come when the weak will say "I am strong" (verse 10). We do not have to look twice to see a spectacular fulfillment of this prophecy in recent times, as far as the political situation is concerned. The past few years have been characterized by the weaker nations of earth asserting themselves against the superpowers. The primary application, of course, will take place in the future when even the weakest nations will join the confederacy Satan forms against Christ and His people. This great gathering leads to executive judgment. At that time the Lord will thrust in His sickle to reap the harvest of the earth.

Satan's Last-Hour Persecutions

When Joel first made these predictions of a last-day confederacy that would be overcome by Christ at His coming, his hearers naturally supposed that these prophecies would apply literally to ancient Israel. Why were they never fulfilled for Israel as a nation?

"A spiritually revived people of Israel, cooperating with God's plan, would have enjoyed the favor and protection of Heaven. The blessings promised at the time of the Exodus (Deut. 28:1-14) would have met belated fulfillment. The Jewish nation would have become a marvel of prosperity and would have converted multitudes to the true God. As the numbers increased, Israel would have enlarged its borders until it embraced the world (see *Christ's Object Lessons*, p. 290). Naturally such a program would have excited the anger of the heathen nations. Under the leadership of Satan these nations would have banded together to crush the thriving state, and God would have intervened" (*The Seventh-day Adventist Bible Commentary*, vol. 4, p. 948).

But the Jews failed to fulfill God's purpose. In spite of the messages God sent through Joel and the other prophets, they never experienced the kind of revival that would enable God to have used them to finish His work on earth.

"With the failure of the Jews, we look to the fulfill-ment of these predictions in principle in the Christian church. . . . The conflict here described will take on the nature of a desperate attempt by Satan, in earth's last hour, to destroy the true church of God. 'As he [Satan] influenced the heathen nations to destroy Israel, so in the near future he will stir up the wicked powers of earth to destroy the people of God' (*Testimonies*, vol. 9, p. 231; . . .). Again God will intervene in behalf of His people, and at the second coming of Christ, will destroy the wicked" (*ibid.*, pp. 948, 949).

In the trauma the church has been undergoing during the past few years, we can see that Satan is doing everything he can right now to keep God's people from uniting and marching in step to finish God's work. But after the shaking, the church will be united in spirit and purpose. Then Satan will stir up the world to destroy the church.

Signs of the Times

Joel 2:29-31 and 3:15, 16 list several "signs of the times" that will mark the coming of the day of the Lord. Some of these have been fulfilled in historical events such as the darkening of the sun on May 19, 1780 and the falling of the stars on the night of November 12-13, 1833. Other predictions, such as Joel 3:16, apparently take place at the actual coming of Christ. *Early Writings* makes this application of the shaking of the heavens: "I saw that when the Lord said 'heaven' in giving the signs recorded by Matthew, Mark, and Luke, He meant heaven, and when He said 'earth' He meant earth. The powers of heaven are the sun, moon, and stars. They rule in the heavens. The powers of earth are those that rule on the earth. The powers of heaven will be shaken at the voice of God. Then the sun, moon, and stars will be moved out of their places. They will not pass away, but be shaken by the voice of God" (p. 41).

Obviously, that has not taken place yet. The chart that follows presents a list of those signs specified by Joel that take place at the second coming of Christ as outlined in *The Great Controversy*.

Sign	Description	Reference
Pouring out of Spirit	Outpouring of the Latter Rain	pp. 611, 612
Darkness, stars withdraw their shining	A dense blackness, deeper than the darkness of the night, falls on the earth	p. 636
Wonders in earth and heaven	Signs and wonders follow in quick succession	p. 636
The Lord roars out of Zion	God's voice pronounces "It is done"	p. 636
Heavens and earth shake	That voice shakes the heaven and the earth; There is a mighty earthquake	pp. 636, 637

David Cohen, the former editor of *Science Digest*, remarked some time ago that "in the next [several] years doomsday is going to be a very popular subject. . . . There will be an increasing strident chorus that the world is coming to an end, because the year 2000 has great mystical and numerological significance." If ever there was a time when Seventh-day Adventists need to watch and be ready, it is now. According to Bible prophecy, doomsday is near. Consequently, Satan is trying to confuse the issue by filling the air with voices bringing in all kinds of deluding interpretations of prophecy. In this way he hopes to discredit genuine apocalyptic expectancy. That would be a tragic loss!

When Satan begins to do everything he can to confuse the world about the second coming of Christ, we can see that he is aware that it must take place soon. In desperation he brings in false teachings to keep the world from being concerned about the Lord's return. But most of all, he attempts to keep the church from being concerned about the Second Coming. He tries to convince us that it is not imminent. In doing this, he seems to be having much more influence among us than he should be having.

Hope for God's People

Notice what God promises to do for His people at the time when the fearful convulsions of nature will be destroying many: "But the Lord will be the hope of his people, and the strength of the children of Israel" (Joel 3:16, last part). The word translated "hope" is the Hebrew word for a refuge or shelter.

Zephaniah 2:1-3 complements this portion of Joel, declaring that there is hope for God's people on the day of the Lord. But that hope depends on our responding to His appeal to turn to Him in full commitment to His plan for us and for the restoration of eternal peace in the world. The proud and stubborn are to seek His meekness and righteousness as the only means of escape from the punishment that has been pronounced on those refusing to heed God's appeal. Then Zephaniah states that those who do so "shall be hid in the day of the Lord's anger."

In chapter 1 we mentioned that the hopeful expression "it may be ye shall be hid" takes on much more certainty in a passage found in *Early Writings*, page 44, where Ellen White states: "God has begun to draw this covering over His people, and it will soon be drawn over all who are to have a shelter in the day of slaughter. God will work in power for His people."

What does it mean to have our feet firmly planted on the truth? It means that we will be so settled in the truth that we cannot be shaken despite all that Satan is doing. When the sealing time is ended and we have survived all Satan's desperate efforts, we not only will have been sealed, but will be covered by God's sheltering protection that will keep us from being harmed by the seven last plagues.

No wonder that Ellen White, when shown the protection and final deliverance of God's people, exclaimed: "Glorious will be the deliverance of those who have patiently waited for His coming and whose names are written in the book of life" (*The Great Controversy*, p. 634).

Where Will We Stand in the Final Judgment?

In the January 10, 1956 *Youth's Instructor*, Dolly Morrison told the story of her father, who emigrated with his parents to America from Russia during the period before the Russian revolution. Although urged by their relatives to become citizens, they delayed doing so, but finally became Americans. Somehow they overlooked the fact that their son, Louis, who was 21, was not covered by their application. Years later he learned that he was not a U.S. citizen. Discouraged about it, he left home and traveled through Europe until he discovered that he could become a citizen. Because of a series of improbable errors, it took a long time for his application to be approved.

Finally Louis appeared in court along with 400 others to be sworn in as citizens of the United States. He waited eagerly for his name to be called: The clerk read "175" and called the name. *Why doesn't he read my name?* Louis wondered, becoming tense. When the clerk reached 350 without calling his name, Louis was sick to his soul. But the clerk went on reading numbers and names, reaching 398, 399, then 400. It was all over. Louis was crushed. The last name had been read, but his had not been called. Rushing to the front, he fell over a chair, but managed to grab the closed book. In agony he cried out, "Why didn't you call my name? Why didn't you?" Weeping uncontrollably, he prostrated himself upon the book from which the names had been read.

The judge ordered the clerk to check the book. When he did so, he found that Louis Morrison's name was second on the list. It had been inadvertently omitted in the reading. When told what had happened, Louis cried out, "Thank God, my name is written in the book!" In a few minutes he was an American citizen.

Soon the all-engrossing question for everyone standing in the valley of decision will be "Is my name written there?" It will be too late then to do anything about it. Now is the time to choose Jesus as our advocate before the judgment throne while the investigative judgment is going on. Only by doing so can we make sure that our names will be written in the Lamb's book of life.

5

"Fill My Cup, Lord"

Because it was a critical time for God's people, the Lord sent the prophets Hosea, Amos, Obadiah, and possibly Joel (see *Prophets and Kings*, p. 108), in addition to Isaiah and Micah, to attempt to prepare the Israelites for the Assyrian invasion and the captivity that followed. Of this group of prophets, Micah seems to have been the youngest.

He is thought to have been a native of the village of Moresheth-gath, located between the hills of the Shephelah and the Philistine plain. Well-known to Christians today for his prediction that the Messiah would be born in Bethlehem (see Micah 5:2), the young prophet nicely complemented the work of Isaiah, presenting the same strong emphasis on ethical standards that characterizes the first part of Isaiah's book.

Coming from a rustic background, Micah seemed most interested in common people and their concerns. He appeals to us as a poet, a lover of nature, and a man of strict integrity. His sternness toward sin was mellowed by a sympathetic and loving interest in the sinner. His themes of condemnation, threat, and judgment were counterbalanced with promises of deliverance and expressions of God's love and mercy.

As is common in the writings of the prophets, Micah

introduced himself briefly in the first verse of his book. Because he mentioned only the kings of Judah, it is assumed that he was a Judean. Assyria was the dominant power in the last part of the eighth century B.C., when Micah was called to the prophetic ministry, so the prophet faced a national spiritual crisis as well as political instability. However, the messages that he and the other prophets presented led to a brief period of reform under good king Hezekiah.

Because the Israelites of Micah's day did not even begin to measure up to what the Lord had made possible for them, the Lord warned them that they would force Him to punish them. God put His case dramatically by summoning all nations to hear what He intended to do in the way of disciplining His people. When we find the kind of overstatements of the extent of God's judgments in the writings of the prophets that we find in chapter 1, they usually indicate that God intended to include more than a warning to the people on whom the judgment was being pronounced. Such hyperbole, as it is called, indicates a last-day application, pointing forward to the time when judgments will fall on the entire world.

Why was God forced to punish Israel and Judah? Micah 1:5 particularly zeroes in on the sins taking place in the "high places." This term refers to the "heathen shrines and sanctuaries erected upon eminences where the inhabitants of Judah practiced their idolatry" (*The Seventh-day Adventist Bible Commentary*, vol. 4, p. 1014).

The northern kingdom of Israel, designated by its capital Samaria, is the first to have its punishment announced (see Micah 1:6), probably because it will be the first to be punished. The last part of verse 7 may be paraphrased this way: "The people were unfaithful to God when they made these idols, and now they will get what their unfaithfulness deserves."

Fortunately, as Christians we do not get what we deserve. Instead, we receive what Christ deserves. "Christ was treated as we deserve, that we might be treated as He deserves. He was condemned for our sins, in which He had no share, that we might be justified by His righteousness, in which we had no share. He suffered the death which was ours, that we might receive the life which was His" (*The Desire of Ages*, p. 25). Those who complain that God does not treat them as they think they should be treated just do not understand *what they deserve*. We should be thankful that God provided a plan of salvation that assures us that not only will we not get what rightfully is ours, but also that we will receive what rightfully is Christ's if we accept Him as our Redeemer.

In verse 8 Micah switched to his own reaction, stating: "I will wail and howl, I will go stripped and naked." By indicating his personal reaction to the announced punishment, Micah attempted to arouse Israel to the terrible consequences that would follow if they persisted in their rebellion against God. The word translated "stripped" is from the Hebrew word that means "barefooted." The word translated "naked" can designate "either complete nakedness or a half-clad condition. Micah represents himself not only as a mourner who removes his outer garments, but also as a captive who is completely stripped of clothing and is carried off naked and despoiled" (*The Seventh-day Adventist Bible Commentary*, vol. 4, p. 1015.)

Israel had filled its cup of iniquity. "Her wound is incurable," God announced through the prophet in verse 9. He then focused His attention on Judah for whom there still was some hope.

Judah Warned

Micah used interesting word plays to describe the punishment that would come on Judah if the people did not repent. These word plays are not apparent in many of the English versions, and not all translators interpret them in the same way, but we can follow Micah's fascinating approach by studying the paraphrase that follows:

Verse 10: Tell it not in Gath (tell town).
             Weep not in [the valley of Baka] (the valley of weeping).
             In the house of Aphrah (dust) roll in the dust.
Verse 11: The inhabitants of Saphir (beautiful) will be naked.
             The inhabitants of Zaanan (come forth) come not forth.
             The wailing of Bethezel (the place at one's side) will take away your standing place.
Verse 12: The inhabitants of Maroth (bitterness) wait anxiously for good.
Verse 13: Harness the horses to the chariots you inhabitants of Lachish (horse town).
Verse 14: Give away the dowry of Moresheth-gath (possessions of Gath).
             The houses of Achzib (lie town) shall be a lie.
Verse 15: I will bring an inheritor who will claim you, Mareshah (inheritance town).
             The glory of Israel shall come to Adullam (shall set forever).

These verses constitute a dirge over the judgment that was to fall on Judah when that nation's cup of iniquity was filled. But Micah concluded this first section of his book with the assurance that there still was a remnant in Judah who served the Lord, and he promised that God would deliver them (see chapter 2:1-11). God has been waiting and longing ever since the inception of sin for His people to do their part so that He can fill their cups with His beneficence rather than with the wrath of punishment.

"Fill my cup, Lord,
I lift it up, Lord!
Come and quench this thirsting of my soul;
Bread of heaven, feed me till I want no more—
Fill my cup, fill it up and make me whole!" *

Our Need for Revival and Reformation

Why is it that so often we seem to fall short too in our Christian experience? Why is it that we do not always enjoy the sparkling, exhilarating joy and peace in our Christian lives that Jesus makes possible? How will we experience the revival we need so much and what has to happen before we can receive the full outpouring of the Holy Spirit in the latter rain?

There can be only one answer as to why we have not received the final outpouring of the Holy Spirit—we do not trust the Lord enough. We pull back life's cup before He can fill it to the brim with the promised outpouring of the Holy Spirit. And the reason we do so is that we are afraid somehow that what *He* has in mind for us is not exactly what we want or think will make us happy.

You know who wrote the twenty-third psalm, don't you? It would be hard to find anyone who has more trouble and sorrow today than David had. Of course, many of his problems were self-inflicted, but that made them even harder to bear. But can you think of anything in the twenty-third psalm which indicates that even David found life filled to overflowing with the blessings that his Good Shepherd poured out on him?

Notice the last part of the verse 5. What does it say? "My cup runneth over." God wants to fill our lives to the

*FILL MY CUP, LORD by Richard Blanchard. © Copyright 1959 by Richard Blanchard, assigned to Sacred Songs. © 1964 Sacred Songs (a div. of Word, Inc.) All Rights Reserved. International Copyright Secured. Used by Permission.

brim with the promised outpouring of the Holy Spirit. But David's blessings and happiness in the Lord did not stop at the brim. His cup was so full that it ran over!

When you're drinking something you enjoy and pass your cup back to ask your hostess to refill it, does she usually fill it to the brim? Probably not. Why not? A person filling a cup usually stops a little below the brim for fear it will spill over. But God is not worried about the blessings and happiness He gives us spilling over. In fact, He *wants* them to!

Because God has *so much more* in mind for us than we want for ourselves, He does not stop at the brim. If we let Him do what He wants to do, He will fill our cups of life so full that they will run over and be a great blessing to those about us.

We Must Empty Our Cups if God Is to Fill Them

One day Jesus gathered the disciples around Him and made it plain to them that the only way He could fill their cups of life was if they first emptied them completely. He told them: "If any man will come after me, let him deny himself, and take up his cross, and follow me. For whosoever will save his life shall lose it: and whosoever will lose his life for my sake shall find it. For what is a man profited, if he shall gain the whole world, and lose his own soul? or what shall a man give in exchange for his soul?" (Matt. 16:24-26).

As you have often heard, it is not in the truest sense an act of self-denial when we yield all we have and are to God. Actually, we deny ourselves when we do not do so. We forfeit that which brings real happiness and satisfaction now and eternally. When I refuse to empty my life of self, I make it impossible for God to fill the cup of my life to overflowing.

Crucifixion was a terrible way to die. Only the worst criminals were put to death that way. Strange as it may seem, the cross, the emblem of the most shameful death possible in the Roman world, has become the glorious emblem of the love of God. When Jesus died on the cross, He decisively defeated sin and death, making eternal life possible for all who choose to take up His cross and follow Him.

"The battle had been won. His right hand and His holy arm had gotten Him the victory. As a conqueror He planted His banner on the eternal heights. Was there not joy among the angels? All heaven triumphed in the Saviour's victory. Satan was defeated, and knew that his kingdom was lost" (*The Desire of Ages*, p. 758).

The glorious fact is that Jesus won that victory for us. Satan is a defeated foe. Even though we still must struggle personally with sin and temptation, our victory is assured if we take full advantage of what Jesus did for us on Calvary.

Overcoming As He Overcame

It should be obvious to each of us by now that we cannot overcome on our own. Our adversary is too strong. But he is a defeated foe. Jesus has gained the victory for us if we will let Him win the battle for us. All that we have to do to is to take full advantage of what Jesus did for us on Calvary.

By the infilling and continual presence of the Holy Spirit from the time He was born, Christ demonstrated the ability of those who are born again to overcome every inherited and cultivated tendency to evil. We are given this insight into His works.

"It is the Spirit that makes effectual what has been wrought out by the world's Redeemer. It is by the Spirit that the heart is made pure. Through the Spirit the believer becomes a partaker of the divine nature. Christ has given His Spirit as a divine power to overcome all hereditary and cultivated tendencies to evil, and to impress His own character upon His church" (*The Desire of Ages*, p. 671).

Some of the ways we cooperate with Jesus in this work of grace are:

1. Avoiding places and situations that we know are likely to tempt us.

2. Overcoming evil habits by replacing them with good habits.

3. Hiding God's Word in our memory to help us recognize His will in every situation.

4. Developing such a great love for Christ that we would rather die than disappoint Him.

5. Being constantly in an attitude of prayer and communion with God.

6. Attending faithfully Sabbath school, church services, and prayer meetings.

7. Organizing prayer and study groups with fellow church members who live in our area.

8. Being faithful in Bible study, and particularly spending some time each day contemplating the life of Jesus.

The Bread of Heaven

Consider the last of these suggestions. The Bible is more popular today than it has ever been. In 1984, 500 million Scripture portions and 15 million complete Bibles were distributed around the world. The Bible has now been translated in more than 1,800 languages. In the United States, Bible sales were up by almost 20 percent. Books about the Bible accounted for more than 40 percent of all Christian books sold. Even though it has been available in English for nearly 600 years, the Bible remains the all-time best-selling book. There is a definite resurgence of interest in the Bible here in the United States. Spiritual leaders in this country speak of an *authentic hunger* on the part of people who feel that something is missing in their spiritual depths.

Recent polls indicate that the majority of Americans believe that the Bible is God's inspired word. Eighty-five percent of American homes have Bibles. But the same polls show that most Americans do not read the Bible regularly. When asked why, most respond that they cannot understand it. According to the pollsters, this includes born-again Christians.

My wife and I enjoy watching the TV game show *Jeopardy!* We have become aware that many contestants seem to avoid selecting any category that has to do with the Bible. They often leave such categories till last, and then they are often unable to answer even the simplest questions.

This illustrates what pollsters have discovered. People today want to know about the Bible—they have a hunger for it—but they do not know much about God's Word or how to understand it. What a tremendous challenge and opportunity this presents to us to launch a last-day crusade of teaching people to understand the Bible! Of course, that means that we must learn to understand it ourselves.

As God's people today we must accept the challenge of letting the Holy Spirit fill the cups of our lives so full that they will run over and bless all with whom we come in contact. When we are filled to overflowing with the bread of heaven, we will have more than enough to share generously with those about us who are hungering for an understanding of the Bible's message for today and are in jeopardy in what Joel calls "the valley of decision" (Joel 3:14).

When we are filled with the Bread of heaven, we also will be able to resist Satan's temptations in the way that Jesus did. When he is tempting and bargaining with us, we will appeal to the "It is written" in God's holy Word as our means of resisting the devil and causing him to flee.

Someday soon every inch of the characters that we have allowed God to build in us will be subjected to minute scrutiny by the Judge of the universe. Because He has promised us unlimited aid in finishing the work of perfecting our characters, we will have no excuse for neglecting any detail, however unimportant it may seem. If we let Him, He will enable us to overcome every cultivated and inherited tendency to evil. That is how great and all-encompassing Christ's victory was. It reaches down to every one of us today, guaranteeing us victory, too—victory over Satan, self, sin, and death.

"My Cup Runneth Over"

When are people the most impressed with our Christianity? Is it when everything is happy, prosperous, and peaceful for us? I don't believe it is. In fact, when everything goes well for us, others may become envious. But what really leads people to desire a religious faith and to want to know and serve Christ better is seeing a Christian going through periods of trial, suffering, sorrow, sickness, and hardship (as David did) and then hearing that person exclaim, "The Lord is *my* Shepherd. . . . My cup runneth over. Surely goodness and mercy will follow me all the days of my life; and I will dwell in the house of the Lord *forever.*"

Contentment and joy even in times of discouragement and trouble—that is true Christian peace! And that is why Psalm 23 is the best-known and best-loved chapter of the Bible. People find so much encouragement in it. When we understand David's experience, we do not at all resent *his* exclaiming, "My cup runneth over." We realize that his testimony came out of a life filled with trials, problems, and personal failures. We recognize that he found special help, special strength, special pleasure, and special joy in the Lord who was his shepherd. But, most of all, we know that *if he, of all people, could, we certainly can too!*

The Lord *wants* to be *our* shepherd today. He longs to pour out His Holy Spirit on us in latter rain power. But it is up to us to let Him do what He longs so much to do. We must empty the cups of our lives of all selfishness and sin and present them to Jesus with the heartfelt petition "Fill my cup, Lord. Fill it so full that I, too, can exclaim 'My cup runneth over.' "

Servant Leadership

In the early 1860s the leaders and constituents of the very youthful "little flock" met to discuss the question of church organization. The venerable Joseph Bates was in the chair, and the keen and sometimes acerbic Uriah Smith acted as secretary and reporter.

Those who spoke to the question included James White, J. N. Loughborough, J. H. Waggoner, J. N. Andrews, M. E. Cornell, and G. I. Butler. Most of the speakers feared that "organization is Babylon," a holdover attitude from 1844. Only James White, John Loughborough, and a layman, Ezra Brackett, were strongly pro-organization, although James White was diplomatically low-key.

Strong-minded men spoke their individual preferences, backed by cogent reasoning. There was much prayer, and a gradual corporate turning toward organization, an imperative if church property was to be properly held and protected. The meeting finally ended in unified agreement, and shortly thereafter the church had a name—Seventh-day Adventist.

We have here an example of leadership at its best—devout men consulting with those whom they lead, expressing diverse opinions, and finally, by God's grace reaching an acceptable solution.

Servant Leaders

It is indeed true that Christ is our leader, but of necessity human beings must act as vice presidents, so to speak.

What, then, is the place of human leadership in the church? In Christ's scheme of things, the one who is "greatest among you shall be your servant" (Matt. 23:11). Administry is to take the place of administration in the church of Christ. The servant-leader is a fellow member of the body of which Christ alone is the head. The servant-leader's position is a significant and influential one, but his or her authority is to be moral rather than kingly. "Servant" in this case does not denote an inferior position, but a willingness to serve others while keeping their best interests in mind. Paul advised the servant-leader Timothy that "the Lord's servant must not quarrel; instead, he must be kind to everyone, able to teach, not resentful. Those who oppose him he must gently instruct, in the hope that God will grant them repentance leading them to a knowledge of the truth" (2 Tim. 2:24, 25, NIV).

Servant leadership, based on moral authority rather than force, is not easy to exercise. It must inspire. It must motivate. It must lead by example. Not only is it more difficult to lead in this manner, but it also takes more time to build confidence and to get people to follow. But when they do follow, they do so from desire rather than from the force of authority.

Ideal servant leadership occurs only when followers recognize the reflection of Christ's character in the leader. They must realize that the leader is dependent upon Christ's will and way in all things and is motivated only by love for Christ and people. That is why God treated Moses' momentary lapse of self-control as such a serious matter. Moses gave a false impression of the character of the leadership of God over His people.

Competence, training, business skills, intelligence, and professionalism are useful in a leader, but all pale into insignificance when contrasted with Christlikeness as a qualification.

Micah's Challenge

Because immorality and lack of integrity in a leader can be devastating to God's people, Micah pointedly challenged the leaders of his day to measure up to their God-given responsibility. He drove this lesson home by denouncing in no uncertain terms their injustice and oppression.

Throughout history there probably have been many more corrupt rulers than those who seem to be characterized by integrity and justice. Today most people are not surprised when their rulers behave in a corrupt fashion. But God had something else in mind for those who ruled His people. They "were called to be the representatives of God to the nation. . . . They should have given to the people an example of integrity and compassion. . . . But this they did not do. Avarice had hardened their hearts" (*The Desire of Ages*, pp. 156, 157).

The utter corruption of the rulers of Israel and Judah was such in Micah's time that the Lord, speaking through His chosen instrument, charged them with *hating* the good and *loving* the evil. The prophet also accused them of being cannibalistic in nature, plucking the skin from those over whom they ruled, and the "flesh from off their bones" (Micah 3:2). Micah obviously was greatly offended at the injustice of the rulers of his day.

The leaders of Israel had been given explicit instructions concerning their behavior. God had given it, point by point, through His servant Moses. These high standards are recorded for us in Deuteronomy 17:15-

20. They can be adapted easily to modern-day leadership.

The leader should be chosen by God. Nowadays the church relies on earnest prayer and the consultation of many God-fearing individuals in making such a choice.

The king, or leader, should not be obsessed with strengthening his position. Deuteronomy 17:16 refers to this practice as multiplying horses to himself.

Neither was the leader to multiply wives to himself. Both David and Solomon transgressed this command. Today we expect our church leaders to set an example of strong, happy family living.

Now, as then, we do well to be uncomfortable with a leader who specializes in personal business acumen.

It was expected that the leader in ancient Israel would "write himself a duplicate" of the law. By making such a "copy" he would show faith in God's Word, and his decision to be guided by it. At that time, as well as now, constant relying on and referring to the Word of God acted as a barrier against avarice, the abuse of power, and myriad other pitfalls common to leadership.

The Problem of Rebellion

In a sinful world, leadership often becomes the point on which deviation, if not outright rebellion, focuses. Paul spoke of this in Romans 16:17, when he warned the brethren to be alert for those who would cause division and throw up roadblocks in the form of deviations from the teachings given by God.

The Seventh-day Adventist Church and its leaders have been plagued by dissident groups almost since the beginning. As early as 1853 the Messenger party directed untrue criticism toward James White, accusing him of dishonest financial dealings.

Their paper, the *Messenger of Truth*, was circulated to *Review* readers, some of whom accepted the contents as gospel truth. In writing of the party and its paper, J. N. Loughborough penned words that aptly describe many dissident groups and their publications from the 1850s to our own time. He said, "The mission of this sheet and its conductors seemed to be to tear down and defame instead of to build up" (*The Great Second Advent Movement*, p. 325).

Common accusations against the church and its leadership are

1. that church organization is getting in the way of doing the Lord's work.

2. that the "storehouse" where the tithe is to be received should not be limited to the denominational treasury.

3. that the General Conference is no longer to be considered the "voice of God on earth."

Attacks on these points represent Satan's attempts to discredit the church and to keep it from fulfilling its God-appointed mission.

"We are living in a solemn time. Satan and evil angels are working with mighty power, with the world on their side to help them. And professed Sabbathkeepers, who profess to believe solemn, important truth, unite their forces with the combined influence of the powers of darkness to distract and tear down that which God designs to build up. The influence of such is recorded as of those who retard the advance of reform among God's people. There are many restless spirits who will not submit to discipline, system, and order. They think their liberties would be abridged were they to lay aside their own judgment and submit to the judgment of those of experience. The work of God will not progress unless there is a disposition to submit to order" (Ellen G. White letter 32, 1892 [see also *Testimonies*, vol. 1, pp. 271, 413]).

Today, God's church has come under heavy criticism from all sides. We would expect that. We are in the shaking time, and Ellen White tells us again and again that everything that can be shaken will be shaken. It is not a pleasant time for the church, but we need to be aware that this shaking is necessary in order to prepare the church for the latter rain and the loud cry that soon will follow.

One black thread binds dissidents together. It is woven into the very fabric of their way of life. They are hypercritical of the church, its beliefs, and its leadership. They are "accusers of the brethren." If only the energy they expend in soul destroying would be spent in soul saving, what a kinder, gentler, more unified church we would have! How much more effective our united witness would be to those searching for the love of Christ!

Elder Cyril Miller puts it this way: "Today the Seventh-day Adventist Church faces a dilemma. It is at odds with itself. The church is constantly being challenged by attacks against its appointed leadership, governance structure, doctrinal positions, prophetic guidance, evangelistic mission, and system of finance. It is under attack from both the liberal left and the radical right. . . .

"It appears that the extremists on the right want to reform the church (and it needs some reformation) while the extremists on the left seek to liberate the church (and it needs some liberation.)

"Unfortunately, the liberals on the left look at the extremists on the right and judge the main body of the church to be legalistic, tradition-bound, and lacking in progressive faith. On the other hand, the radicals on the right, observing the extremists on the far left, judge the main body to be compromising, worldly, and departing from the faith. . . .

"True, you can be a Seventh-day Adventist and still

lean a little to the left or recline a little to the right. Perhaps most of us do in one way or another. However, when you go too far you cross a line where you cease to be a Seventh-day Adventist. Many who do this, end up in total opposition to the church and wonder why" ("Keepers of the Springs," *Journal of the Adventist Theological Society*, Spring 1990, pp. 119, 120).

How Do We Meet the Challenges Outlined Above?

Challenge 1. Church organization is getting in the way of doing the Lord's work.

Jesus designed a simple church structure. At the center were the 12 who attended His open-air seminary for approximately three years. Beyond that were the 70 set apart for service and organized into 35 missionary teams for door-to-door and village-to-village medical missionary work (see Luke 10). Then there were the 500 who met with Him in Galilee after His resurrection (see Matt. 28:16-20; 1 Cor. 15:6). Also, 120 gathered in Jerusalem before Pentecost (Acts 1:15). All were commissioned missionaries.

From the beginning, the mission of the church has been the salvation of souls. That still is the clear, simple purpose for which the church exists. "Its mission is to carry the gospel to the world. From the beginning it has been God's plan that through His church shall be reflected to the world His fullness and His sufficiency" (*The Acts of the Apostles*, p. 9).

We should never lose sight of the fact that this is the charter and the reason for existence of the church today. Church organization is essential in carrying on God's work.

Christ is the head of the church. As such He ultimately is responsible for the setting up and removing of the leaders of the church. It is not our business to do this work. He sometimes is much more patient than we would be. Therefore we should be fearful of attacking and criticizing the Lord's anointed, just as David was. When we attack the church and its leadership, we are attacking that upon which Christ bestows His supreme regard. In fact, when we attack church leadership we are attacking Christ, for He is the "head."

Challenge 2. The "storehouse" where tithe should be received should not be limited to the denominational treasury.

The tithing practice, like the Sabbath, was established in the Old Testament, and its validity was assured in the New Testament. No one has the right to change either, unless God specifically indicates an exception. Ellen White upheld the Bible principle that the tithe was to be used for the support of the divinely ordained ministry of God's organized work. It is true that at one time the Lord instructed her to support some ministers and their wives working with the Southern Missionary Society, who were in desperate need, with tithe money (1900-1906), *before* the organization made provisions for such needs. Even though these workers were denominationally-recognized ministers working in harmony with the conference, the Lord did not instruct others to follow her practice to meet emergency or normal needs.

Ellen White recognized the "storehouse" or "treasure house of God" as being the source set up in the church from which the ministers receive their monthly checks. Ministers are to teach their members that this is God's appointed storehouse (see *Testimonies*, vol. 9, p. 250; *Evangelism*, p. 250).

Challenge 3. The General Conference no longer is to be considered the "voice of God on earth."

In the early 1900s Ellen White wrote against "kingly power" and "Jerusalem centers" and urged decentralization of power in the church. When she wrote, there was one president and one vice president in the General Conference, and 13 members on the General Conference Committee. The latest *SDA Yearbook* indicates that about 55 people are listed as General Conference administrators and 400 as members of the General Conference Committee. These men and women represent every part of the globe and every aspect of our work. The instruction God gave the church at that time regarding decentralizing power has been carried out. A later Ellen White statement clarifies the issue: "At times, when a small group of men entrusted with the general management of the work have, in the name of the General Conference, sought to carry out unwise plans and to restrict God's work, I have said that I could no longer regard the voice of the General Conference, represented by these few men, as the voice of God. But this is not saying that the decisions of a General Conference composed of an assembly of duly appointed representative men from all parts of the field should not be respected" (*Testimonies*, vol. 9, pp. 260, 261, written in 1909).

Those who claim that Ellen White did not believe after 1901 that the General Conference has been given authority by God and serves as His voice on earth completely distort her position.

Sins of False Prophets Denounced

The leading sin of the false leaders, as stated in Micah 3:5, is that they were making people err, or sin. How great is the guilt of one who leads others from the true path!

Micah refers to spiritual darkness that envelops these people. Their lying theme is "peace," when the situation is going from bad to worse.

The truth-seeking follower of God must be wise and alert in discerning false leadership, and thereby be protected from its ravages.

It is not always easy to see through false claims. Once, when Henry VI of England went on a pilgrimage to a shrine at St. Albans, a beggar, claiming to have been born blind, announced to the king that all of a sudden he could see. The church bells rang out in celebration of the miracle. But Duke Humphrey of Gloucester, who was accompanying the king, became skeptical of the beggar's claim.

Summoning the man, he asked him if he really had been blind from birth. Both the beggar and his wife assured the duke that such was the case. Humphrey advised him to give the glory to God. Then, peering intently into the beggar's eyes, he said to him, "I believe you very well that you were born blind, for me thinketh that you cannot see well yet."

"Oh, but sir," the beggar responded, "I can see now as well as any man."

"Then what color is my gown?" the duke asked. In order to show how well he could see, the beggar not only told the duke the color of his gown, but gave an accurate description of the colors of all the gowns around him.

Duke Humphrey had him locked in the stocks, explaining that "though he could have seen suddenly by a miracle the differences between diverse colors, yet he could not suddenly be able to tell the names of those colors."

The last-day deceptions and miracles worked by Satan and his agents will be so subtle that, if possible, they will deceive the very elect. We will need more than human wisdom to be able to keep from being deceived. Particularly deceptive will be those who come from leadership positions in our own ranks to spread false theories and deceitful doctrines.

But we cannot let the fact that there have been and will be false leaders turn us against the God-appointed leadership of His people. Remember that it is Christ who is our true leader and that it is His responsibility to provide us with the right kind of servant leadership. Now, when the leadership of the church is calling us to revival and reformation, they have the responsibility of showing us the way through their own commitment and example. But we have the responsibility of "follow-ship." We must each play our God-assigned role in preparing for and participating in the last great revival God is bringing to His people.

7

Promises of Hope

Micah 4 contains a promise of restoration and Micah 5 contains the spectacular prediction, written 700 years before the event, that the Messiah would be born in the little town of Bethlehem. In a world of crisis and despair, these ancient predictions still offer promises of hope for those now living on this doomed planet.

The prediction in Micah 3:12 of Jerusalem's destruction and of Zion being plowed as a field is followed in chapters 4 and 5 by the glorious promises of restoration through the Messiah, who will at last become the ruler of the New Jerusalem. Often in the writings of the prophets, predictions of doom on those who are evil are followed by promises of restoration to those who are faithful. Of course, these predictions to Judah were conditional on their cooperation with God's plan and their acceptance of the Messiah. Because they rejected the Messiah, the prophecies never were fulfilled to them in the ultimate sense. However, the unfulfilled portions of these prophecies point to a fulfillment yet to take place in "the latter days"—the days in which we live—to the remnant of God's people who are getting ready for Jesus' second coming.

In Bible prophecy the term "the latter days" or "the last days" is "used of: (1) the end of the power of Greece

(Dan. 8:23); (2) the close of the 1260 and 2300 days (Dan. 10:14; 8:19); (3) the ingathering of the Gentiles at the close of the age (Isa. 2:2; Micah 4:1); (4) the battle of Gog and Magog immediately prior to the establishment of the Messianic kingdom (Eze. 38:6, 7, 16); (5) the great day of final judgment (Jer. 23:20; 30:24); (6) the final 'end' of the wicked (Ps. 37:38)" (*The Seventh-day Adventist Bible Commentary*, vol. 4, p. 103).

To us, of course, the significance of the unfulfilled prophecies of the Old Testament is that many are to be fulfilled today in the events that surround the second coming of Christ. Anyone who is aware of the ongoing crisis in the Middle East and the dramatic changes taking place elsewhere in this world recognizes that these are interesting and fascinating times. What is happening can best be understood in connection with the promises of hope outlined in Bible prophecy.

Two Prophecies Compared

If you will take time to open your Bible and compare Micah 4:1-5 with Isaiah 2:1-5, you will notice immediately that there are some very clear parallels and similarities, as well as a few notable differences. For a long time Bible scholars have been discussing the question of whether Isaiah copied from Micah or Micah copied from Isaiah. Some have taken the position that they both received original revelations of the same material. The fact that Isaiah introduces his readers to "the word that Isaiah the son of Amoz saw concerning Judah and Jerusalem" (Isa. 2:1) indicates that the parallels often noted between this section of Micah and Isaiah's similar passage could be attributed originally to Isaiah. If so, Micah, operating under the inspiration of the Holy Spirit, adapts it to fit his own context. Although verse 4 of Micah 4 is not found in Isaiah 2, it reflects Isaiah 65:17-25.

Of more specific interest to us today are the implications found in these prophecies concerning the political events now taking place in such a rapid and astounding way. As of this writing, much of the prophecy of Micah 4 has not yet taken place, but events in the Middle East point toward its fulfillment. Whereas the major fulfillment of this prophecy will occur in the earth made new, current conditions indicate that we are living in a time when people and nations are attempting to "beat their swords into plowshares," desperately hoping to avoid war in spite of continued outbreaks of conflict.

But in the New Jerusalem, after the great battle at the end of the millennium, will be ushered in the only possible period of true peace under the always-beneficent and munificent reign of our Lord and eternal King. Only then will it be possible for every man to sit "under his fig tree" without anyone ever making them afraid again (see Micah 4:4). The reason given for the advent of eternal peace is that "we will walk in the name of the Lord our God for ever and ever" (verse 5), and "the Lord shall reign over them in mount Zion" (verse 7).

Application to Our Day

Ellen White indicates how the final fulfillment of the promises of Micah 4 will take place: "The present is a time of overwhelming interest to all living. Rulers and statesmen, men who occupy positions of trust and authority, thinking men and women of all classes, have their attention fixed upon the events taking place about us. They are watching the relations that exist among the nations. They observe the intensity that is taking possession of every earthly element, and they recognize that something great and decisive is about to take place—that the world is on the verge of a stupendous crisis.

"The Bible, and the Bible only, gives a correct view of these things. Here are revealed the great final scenes in the history of our world, events that already are casting their shadows before, the sound of their approach causing the earth to tremble and men's hearts to fail them for fear" (*Prophets and Kings*, p. 537).

Then, after quoting, among other prophecies, Micah 4:10-12, she adds: "God will not fail His church in the hour of her greatest peril. He has promised deliverance. . . . Then will the purpose of God be fulfilled, the principles of His kingdom will be honored by all beneath the sun" (*ibid.*, p. 538).

Today we are on the "verge of a stupendous crisis." The key word that identifies the major sign of our times is *intensity*. When in the course of human history has there been such intensity in the fulfillment of the signs of Christ's coming?

God has promised not to fail His church. The promises and purposes of God will soon be fulfilled. But that raises another question. Will we as a church fail God? We dare not do so as we witness the fast-fulfilling of the signs of our times.

The Messiah Promised

The "last day" prophecies of chapter 4 naturally lead into the Messianic prophecy of chapter 5. From our perspective, we tend to separate the two because we know that Jesus came nearly 2,000 years ago. However, if the Jews had responded the way that God wanted them to, the coming of the Messiah would have ushered in the final events that we include in the term "last days." So, rightly, the people of Christ's day made no such distinction as do we from our perspective.

Commenting on the familiar prophecy of Micah 5:2, *The SDA Bible Commentary* states that Bethlehem is a town "5 1/4 mi. (8.4 km.) south of Jerusalem. . . . The town was also called Ephrath (Gen. 35:19; cf. Ruth 4:11) and Bethlehem-judah, doubtless to distinguish it from Bethlehem in Zebulun. . . . 'Little' may . . . refer either to the clan represented by the inhabitants of Bethlehem or possibly to the town itself, which never assumed very great importance" (vol. 4, p. 1024).

Jesus may have had the words of the last part of Micah 5:2 in mind when He solemnly announced to the Jews, "Truly, truly, I say to you, before Abraham was, I am" (John 8:58, RSV).

Notice what happened when He made that statement: "Silence fell upon the vast assembly. The name of God, given to Moses to express the idea of the eternal presence, had been claimed as His own by this Galilean Rabbi. He had announced Himself to be the self-existent One, He who had been promised to Israel, 'whose goings forth have been from of old, from the days of eternity' (Micah 5:2, margin).

"Again the priests and rabbis cried out against Jesus as a blasphemer. His claim to be one with God had before stirred them to take His life. . . . Because He was, and avowed Himself to be, the Son of God, they were bent on destroying Him. Now many of the people, siding with the priests and rabbis, took up stones to cast at Him. 'But Jesus hid Himself, and went out of the temple, going through the midst of them, and so passed by' " (*The Desire of Ages*, pp. 469, 470).

Apparently, Micah's prophecy helped Jesus identify His divinity and His mission. But he was not the first to do so. The strangest part of the story of the Wise Men from the East who found Jesus in Bethlehem is that those considered to be the wisest people in Jerusalem at that time did not bother seeking Him, thus they did not find Him. These scholars knew exactly where Christ was to be born. They told the Wise Men where to find Him. But they were not interested enough to take a look for themselves. Why? They were so wise in their own conceit that they ended up becoming ridiculed for all time as the most foolish men of their day.

We live in a time when most of the "wisest" individuals of our world still scoff at the story of Bethlehem. But the truly wise will find Him and worship Him—recognizing Him as the king who came down to us so that we might spend all eternity with Him in His kingdom of glory.

The Promises Are for Us

Today many in our world are confused by the rapid pace of events. The status quo and stability they were counting on have disappeared to a great extent. The very earth on which they live threatens to turn on them and destroy them.

When things seem the most hopeless, we need to cling to God's promises for the future. How God works in seemingly hopeless situations is illustrated by the story of the Kuwamotos, who lived in Hiroshima, Japan. Mrs. Kuwamoto considered her husband to be a hopeless case until the first atomic bomb exploded over her city. She was working in the kitchen while her husband entertained a friend who had dropped by early that morning. When the atomic bomb exploded 1,850 feet in the air over the city, the Kuwamotos' home collapsed, burying them all. Mrs. Kuwamoto was badly shaken, but managed to crawl out from under the wreckage. She was able to pull out their visitor from under some debris, but Mr. Kuwamoto was trapped under a heavy beam. No matter how hard she pulled and tugged, she could not release her husband.

Heat rays from the bomb, with temperatures of more than 3,000 degrees Celsius, combined with cooking fires in the destroyed houses to cause devastating firestorms that swept the city. The fire was racing toward what had been the Kuwamoto home. Mr. Kuwamoto realized that he was doomed. Then and there the most serious conversation the Kuwamotos ever had took place. Up until then he had refused to listen as his wife urged him to make things right with God so that he could be assured of a place in heaven. Now for the first time he was fearfully interested. He confessed his sins and stubbornness to his wife. He told her that now he knew what she had been trying to teach him through the years was true. He wanted to be forgiven and asked her to pray with him that they might be together in heaven. After they had prayed together, he insisted that she leave him and flee for her life. It was a terrible ordeal for her to leave her life companion to die while she fled. But he continued to insist on it, so she did.

The next day Kuwamoto-san picked her way through the smoldering embers of the destroyed city. Blackened corpses were strewn everywhere. It was difficult to get her bearings and identify her home. When she finally did, she saw that her home had been completely destroyed. All her earthly possessions were gone. She found the remains of her husband, knelt silently in prayer, and committed him to the Father above, thankful that through the terrible ordeal he had been saved at last.

That's what counts most in days like these. We must have the blessed hope that we will be saved at last.

What God Expects

Unfortunately, we live in a time when people are turning to the courts to settle their problems rather than attempting to work out their differences in the way the Bible suggests. As a consequence our courts are flooded with cases, and the analogy of the court case that we find in the sixth chapter of Micah is quite familiar to many of us.

In this chapter God summons Israel into a figurative court of law in order that His case against them might be judged by neutral parties. They, of course, do not stand a chance of winning the case because they do not understand God well enough to appreciate how He has related to them, what He has done for them, or even the meaning of the prescribed sacrifices that He has given for their spiritual development.

Because the surrounding mountains and hills have witnessed both God's goodness and His gracious dealings with the nation as well as the people's ingratitude and rebelliousness, God calls on these inanimate witnesses to serve as an impartial, yet knowledgeable jury.

The Essence of God's Case

In chapter 6, verse 3, Micah sets forth God's challenge to His people to testify what He has done that has "wearied" them. In doing so, he echoes Isaiah, his contemporary. The fifth chapter of Isaiah portrays Israel as a well-tended and cared-for vineyard. After having done all He could to assure the best vineyard possible, God challenged the people to judge between Him and His vineyard, asking, "What more could I have done that I have not done?"

What did God say He had done for His people? According to Isaiah 5, He placed them "in a very fruitful hill"—He put them in the land of Canaan, a place flowing with milk and honey. He "fenced" His vineyard—He gave them His law as a protection about them. He "gathered out the stones"—He removed their idolatrous neighbors. He "planted it with the choicest vine"—He put His people there. He "built a tower in the midst of it"—the Temple. He "also made a winepress therein"—"This may be thought of as representing institutions like the schools of the prophets, which were God's appointed means for inculcating such virtues and graces as righteousness, justice, honesty, and purity" (*The Seventh-day Adventist Bible Commentary*, vol. 4, p. 122).

What more could God have done? He had done everything He possibly could up to that point to enable them to bring forth a beautiful crop of righteousness. But what happened? Instead of the fruit of the Spirit, they brought forth the fruits of the flesh—"wild grapes."

"God desired to make of His people Israel a praise and a glory. Every spiritual advantage was given them. God withheld from them nothing favorable as to the formation of character that would make them representatives of Himself" (*Christ's Object Lessons*, p. 288).

Although at that point in time God was not able to do anything more for Israel, later He *was* able to do much more. In recounting this parable, Jesus added, "Last of all he sent unto them his son" (Matt. 21:37). How did they respond to this even greater benefit? They "cast him out of the vineyard, and slew him" (verse 39).

That left God with no recourse but to let His vineyard, Israel, wither away.

What God Wants

The prophet Micah presented the Lord's challenge to take the matter to a great universal court of law. The Lord dared the people to show that He had failed them.

What did Micah have to say about the way the people responded to God's challenge? It was most inadequate. In fact, they seemed to be ignorant about God's true nature and about what He requires and why He requires it.

What did the people seem to think that God wanted most from them? Some suggestions were: bowing before the Lord, bringing burnt offerings, bringing Him thousands of rams or 10,000 rivers of oil, or even offering their firstborn (see Micah 6:6, 7).

The answer, of course, to the question of what God expects is "None of these." In their response the people moved from the minimal, the burnt offering, to what they considered to be the maximum, the offering of their sons and daughters. But they did not seem to understand that God was not content with their offerings. He wanted *them*. For their part, the people seemed to be willing to give God almost anything but themselves.

God desires His people to let Him come in and take over their hearts. The results of yielding completely to Him will be seen in their attitude and behavior.

What does God say in verse 8 that He expects from His people? The words "He hath shewed thee" indicate that the people Micah addressed already were aware of God's requirements. Yet because they seemed to have forgotten what God expected, the Lord had to remind them many times about what constitutes true religion. The attributes Micah listed are Godlike in quality, indicating that we are to reflect His justice and loving-kindness and to walk circumspectly as though always in His presence. There are three main things God desires of His people:

1. *"To do justly"* — "The objective of true religion is character development. Outward ceremony is of value only as it contributes to such development. But because it is often easier to render outward service than to change the evil propensities of the heart, men have ever been more ready to render external worship than to cultivate the graces of the soul. . . .

" 'To do justly . . .' is to act with justice and kindness. These are manward virtues and sum up the intent of the second table of the Decalogue" (*The Seventh-day Adventist Bible Commentary*, vol. 4, p. 1028).

In *The Grace of Giving*, Stephen Olford illustrates what it means to do justly by telling the story of a Baptist pastor, Peter Miller, who lived in Ephrata, Pennsylvania, during the American Revolution. Miller happened to be a friend of George Washington.

A man named Michael Wittman also lived in Ephrata. He was an evil-minded sort who did all he could to oppose and humiliate the pastor.

One day Michael Wittman was arrested for treason and sentenced to die. Peter Miller traveled 70 miles on foot to Philadelphia to plead for the life of the traitor.

"No, Peter," General Washington said. "I cannot grant you the life of your friend."

"My friend!" exclaimed the old preacher. "He's the bitterest enemy I have."

"What?" cried Washington. "You've walked 70 miles to save the life of an enemy? That puts the matter in a different light. I'll grant the pardon." And he did.

Peter Miller took Michael Wittman back home to Ephrata—no longer an enemy but a friend.

2. *"To love mercy"* —In Philippians 2, Paul tells us

how Jesus emptied Himself for us, holding back nothing. He gave Himself freely, fully, and joyfully. That is what true mercy is all about—Jesus' kind of love and mercy. This becomes the distinguishing mark of the true Christian. Why is it so essential?

"There are many to whom life is a painful struggle; they feel their deficiencies and are miserable and unbelieving; they think they have nothing for which to be grateful. Kind words, looks of sympathy, expressions of appreciation, would be to many a struggling and lonely one as a cup of cold water to a thirsty soul. A word of sympathy, an act of kindness, would lift burdens that rest heavily upon weary shoulders. And every word or deed of unselfish kindness is an expression of the love of Christ for lost humanity" (*Thoughts From the Mount of Blessing*, p. 23).

In the Beatitudes, Jesus added to the blessing on the merciful the promise "For they shall obtain mercy" (Matt. 5:7). By exercising the muscles of unselfishness, we reap the results of merciful love. We do not lose anything when we share our blessings with those about us. As we give, we gain. That is a law of life.

3. *"To walk humbly with thy God"*—The story is told about how the ancient Christian known as Saint Anthony went into the desert to live in solitude in order to become perfect through self-denial. There he had become very much satisfied with himself. One day as he spoke aloud his conviction that he was the most saintly person on earth, he heard what he recognized to be God's voice.

"No, Anthony. Cobbler Conrad in Jerusalem is more saintly than you."

"What does he do that I do not do?" Anthony demanded.

"Go and discover for yourself what that is," the Lord replied.

Making his way to Jerusalem, Anthony found the humble shop of Conrad the cobbler. When Anthony asked him what he had done that made the Lord look upon him as being a greater saint than he, the cobbler answered, "I have done little but sit here and mend the shoes that are brought to me. But I mend each pair of shoes and sandals as though each belonged to Christ Himself. That is all I do. That may not be much."

It is said that Anthony bowed his head humbly and departed, determined to return where people were and to serve them as he would serve the Lord.

When we are willing to humble ourselves, to empty ourselves in order to be empty vessels to hold the mercies of God and to walk humbly in the path of service, the Lord will be able to use us. He will fill us full of blessings to bestow on those about us.

The little girl's prayer, "Dear Lord, make all the bad people good, and all the good people kind," presents a real challenge to us to reveal fully the love and goodness of Christ.

Ellen White enlarges on Micah's challenge to practical Christian living: "An adherence to the strictest principles of truth will frequently cause present inconvenience and may even involve temporal loss, but it will increase the reward in the future life. Religion does not consist merely in a system of dry doctrines, but in practical faith, which sanctifies the life and corrects the conduct in the family circle and in the church. Many may tithe mint and rue, but neglect the weightier matters, mercy and the love of God. To walk humbly with God is essential to the perfection of Christian character. God requires undeviating principle in the minutest details of the transactions of life. Said Christ, 'He that is faithful in that which is least is faithful also in much' " (*Testimonies*, vol. 4, p. 337).

What About Us?

As mentioned at the beginning of this chapter, God is pictured in Micah 6 as summoning Israel into a figurative court of law. He called on the surrounding mountains and hills, as neutral parties, to judge His case against His people. The people did not stand a chance of winning the contested case. They had no real understanding of all that God had done and was continuing to do for them.

We may wonder at their blindness and hardheartedness. But do we have room for criticizing them? In the light of all that God has done for us and in the light of the fact that we stand this side of Calvary, how would we answer His charges of apathy and rebelliousness if we found ourselves facing an impartial jury in the court of the universe?

After God clearly outlined what He expected of His people, He pointed out how far short the people to whom He sent Micah came of fulfilling His expectations. Therefore, the judgment to be pronounced on them would be well-deserved. Nevertheless, even then, there were a few who were "wise" and who responded to God's presentation of His case and repented of their evil ways. The same is true of the church and its people today.

The all-important question is What does God expect of us? The answer is No more than He has made possible for us to do and to be. Do we really understand what that is?

CHAPTER

9

"Woe Is Me!"

Many commentators believe that Micah was speaking in behalf of Israel in chapter 7 of his book. However, the passage can be also understood as being the prophet's account of his personal experience. It cannot be denied that Micah had the broader view in mind, but neither should we overlook the personal aspect of this intriguing chapter. In the light of Israel's indifferent response to the message that the Lord sent him to present, we might expect Micah to become discouraged and frustrated.

But the book does not end with the portrait of a discouraged prophet. Micah looked to the Lord, realized his own sinfulness and need, and turned to the Lord in deep repentance for his own lack of faith.

In his characteristic manner of using figures of speech, Micah portrayed himself, as well as his people, as being as dried up and desolate as a vineyard would appear after the harvest. He felt so barren that he cried out "Woe is me!" just as Isaiah did in his time of discouragement. These personal reactions demonstrate the humanity of the prophets. In the midst of prophetic thunderings they still showed human reactions.

It is not easy for a prophet to have to point out continually the sins of his people, as Micah was commissioned to do. In chapter 3:8 the prophet relates that he has been given power through the Holy Spirit "to declare to Jacob his transgression and to Israel his sin" (RSV). After years of this kind of essential but often-critical ministry, it is no wonder that his soul would tend to dry up.

Micah viewed the people about him as being so eager to work iniquity that they "do evil with both hands earnestly" (Micah 7:3). In what might be a commentary on our day, he mentioned how "the prince and the judge ask for a bribe, and the great man utters the evil desire of his soul" (verse 3, RSV).

In his disillusionment the prophet could not trust anyone, not even the members of his own family. In what seems the height of cynicism, he cautioned, "Guard the doors of your mouth from her who lies in your bosom" (verse 5, RSV). Such a comment makes us wonder what kind of wife he had.

An Abrupt Change

However, something special took place between verse 6 and verse 7 that turned Micah's attention away from the terrible condition of those about him to a concentration on the Lord. Perhaps he had the same kind of theophany or vision of God that Isaiah had.

A careful comparison of Micah's experience outlined in chapter 7:1-10 with that of Isaiah recorded in chapter 6:1-10 of his book reveals the similarities as well as the differences of their experience.

Question	Micah	Isaiah
At what point in his experience did the prophet exclaim "Woe is me"?	After years of seemingly fruitless ministry	When he saw his need in his vision early in his ministry
What led to the despondent condition of the prophet?	Dwelling on the sins of his people	Same
What happened to change the prophet's experience?	He caught a vision of God's holiness	Same
What did the prophet realize that enabled him to be more sympathetic to the people?	His own sinfulness and need of forgiveness	Same
What was the result in the prophet's ministry?	He became more understanding and effective	Same

About to give up his ministry, Isaiah went into the court of the Temple. Standing outside the Temple proper, he was able to see the great inner veil. Suddenly the embroidered angels on the veil came to life before his startled eyes. No longer did Isaiah find himself peering into the earthly sanctuary. Instead, he was given the tremendous privilege of looking into God's temple in heaven. What a thrilling scene he describes!

"I saw the Lord sitting upon a throne, high and lifted up; and his train filled the temple. Above him stood the seraphim; each had six wings: with two he covered his face, and with two he covered his feet, and with two he flew. And one called to another and said: 'Holy, holy, holy is the Lord of hosts; the whole earth is full of his glory' " (Isa. 6:1-3, RSV).

How did Isaiah respond? As indicated above, with the same words Micah used. But there was a difference. Isaiah cried out "Woe is me!" as he began to recognize that he himself was not right with God, that he was a man of sinful (probably critical) lips. The people had the same problem. But Isaiah, who had condemned them as being so sinful that they were sick from the soles of their feet to the top of their head (see Isa. 1:5, 6), now recognized that, in comparison with the holiness of God, he wasn't much better than they.

Micah cried out "Woe is me!" as he contemplated the terrible wickedness of the people of his nation. He couldn't find one individual that he considered to be upright. He does not indicate what happened to change his perspective, but all of a sudden he was looking in a different direction. He was looking "unto the Lord" (Micah 7:7). God was in control. He would in His own good time make all things right.

Notice how Micah expressed his new determination concerning his subsequent relationship with the Lord: "I will bear the indignation of the Lord, because I have sinned against him, until he plead my cause, and execute judgment for me: he will bring me forth to the light, and I shall behold his righteousness" (verse 9).

"This is the language of the truly penitent. He realizes that his only hope is in God. He asks for no mitigation of punishment. He knows that whatever God does will be for his good" (*The Seventh-day Adventist Bible Commentary*, vol. 4, p. 1030).

Now the prophet is willing to wait trustingly for the God of salvation to act in the way He knows is best. He could pray as did the psalmist: "Let me not be ashamed; for I put my trust in thee. Let integrity and uprightness preserve me; for I wait on thee" (Ps. 25:20, 21). "I wait for the Lord, my soul doth wait, and in his word do I hope. My soul waiteth for the Lord more than they that watch for the morning. . . . Let Israel hope in the Lord: for with the Lord there is mercy, and with him is plenteous redemption" (Ps. 130:5-7).

One story has it that one day Charles Wesley was sitting by his window looking out at the glories of nature. Suddenly he noticed a hawk swooping down on a small bird. The frightened little creature was doing everything possible to avoid being caught by the hawk, but there did not seem any hiding place. Then it noticed the open window and the man sitting there. Desperate, the bird flew in the window and, with trembling heart, found refuge in Wesley's bosom. This led him to write the comforting hymn:

"Jesus, lover of my soul,
    Let me to Thy bosom fly. . . .
All my trust on Thee is stayed,
    All my help from Thee I bring;
Cover my defenseless head
    With the shadow of Thy wing."

We cannot go wrong if we put our trust completely in the Lord—if we wait patiently on Him, trusting that He will do that which is best for us.

Restoration Recounted

In the remainder of the seventh chapter, Micah focuses on the future restoration of Israel. He sees God as the good shepherd, who will care for and provide for His people. He even notes the surrounding nations turning in dread to the Lord.

When God's people make things right with Him, He makes everything right for them. Micah 7:11 gave Israel the assurance of restoration. After the return from Babylonian captivity, the walls of her cities were rebuilt, but more than that is intended here. The Lord was to become a wall of protection for His people (see Zech. 2:4, 5). The word translated "decree" may also mean "boundary." If this is the sense in which it is used in this verse, it refers to the expansion of Israel's boundaries and influence.

Then we come to the last, incomparable section of this glorious chapter. Micah apparently became a much more sympathetic and understanding preacher after he turned his eyes on the Lord instead of concentrating on the sins of his people. The last notes of this great song are happy and hopeful: "Who is a God like unto thee, that pardoneth iniquity, and passeth by the transgression of the remnant of his heritage? he retaineth not his anger for ever, because he delighteth in mercy. He will turn again, he will have compassion upon us; he will subdue our iniquities, and thou wilt cast all their sins into the depths of the sea" (Micah 7:18, 19).

The prophet, who a little while before had been saying that "the best of them is as a brier: the most upright is sharper than a thorn hedge" (verse 4), now dwells on the assurance that God is willing to forgive their iniquity. How much is He willing to forgive if they will repent? Micah answers, "All their sins." There is no sin that God is not eager and glad and more than willing to forgive if we will turn to Him for forgiveness. Micah ends his book on a triumphant note of God's willingness to faithfully provide for all our needs.

At a recent stop-smoking program, a lady said to me, "Oh, you Adventists are so wonderful, so happy, so healthy! You don't have any hang-ups at all, do you?" How I wish that were true! The point is, it should be true. God has given us all power in heaven and earth through Jesus Christ and the pouring out of the Spirit's power to make us full representatives of His love and character—a group of people known around the world as those who do not have any hang-ups.

Micah and Isaiah had hang-ups, but they learned to take them to the Lord. When they began to focus on the

Lord rather than on people, they not only recognized their own great need, but also found that the Lord was more than willing to supply their needs. God wants to help us and save us much more than we can begin to appreciate.

The following story may help us comprehend how much God wants us to become members of the family of heaven. Baby Freddie was placed in an adoption agency, but because he was born without arms he was put on the "Hard-to-Place" list. Frances and Edwin Pearson came to the agency seeking a child—a boy—to adopt. Mrs. Pearson glanced proudly at her husband, who was very athletic, and said he would be good for a boy.

The Pearsons admitted that they didn't have much money, but Mrs. Pearson insisted, "We've got a lot of love. We've been saving that up!"

The social worker interviewed the couple thoughtfully and then told them that there was one little 13-month-old boy available. The Pearsons were thrilled. Then she produced Freddie's picture, saying, "He's a wonderful little boy, but he was born without arms."

The Pearsons studied the photograph. "He could play kickball," Mrs. Pearson suggested.

"Oh, arms aren't so important. He can get by without them. But a head he couldn't. We can teach him a lot of things," Mr. Pearson chimed in.

"Then you think you might want him?" the lady from the agency asked.

"Might? Might?" the Pearsons responded. "We want him!"

They took Freddie into their home and into their hearts.

God *wants* us. Six thousand years of degeneracy and disfigurement of sin have marred and deformed us. But God still wants us! He wants to take us and make us whole again in the truest sense.

The book *Ministry of Healing* states that "the gospel is a wonderful simplifier of life's problems" (p. 363). If we're having a lot of concerns, what we need is much more of the simplifying gospel, much more of Christ in our lives. The Lord pleads with us, as He did in the days of Micah, "O my people, what have I done to you? In what have I wearied you? Answer me!" (Micah 6:3, RSV). "What more can I do for you than that which I already have done?" He asks. "Come to Me now for deliverance and restoration. Come before it is too late."

CHAPTER

10

—

Crowding Sin
Out of Our Lives

The message of impending judgment that God gave His people through the prophet Zephaniah must have come as quite a shock to those described as being as congealed in their minds as the dregs left after wine making. In today's vernacular we would say that someone taking that attitude seems to be one brick shy of a load! In this thick-headed condition the people of Judah boasted scoffingly, "The Lord will not do good, nor will he do ill" (Zeph. 1:12, RSV). The "thickening upon their lees" referred to the mental attitude that led many of them to feel that they could let down their spiritual guard and relax their religious awareness. In all honesty, do we need to admit that sometimes we still reflect that kind of attitude?

Because of their spiritual lethargy, God had to apply the shock treatment to His people in Zephaniah's day. He still is doing so more than 2,500 years later. The Lord wants us to be aware that we live in the time of investigative judgment. Probation soon will close.

Most of the prophets share little information about themselves. They seem to want to get right into their message. However, in what is the longest genealogy given by the prophets, Zephaniah reveals his family tree. He seems to take pride in his ancestry, as he traces his lineage back four generations to King Hezekiah. This background helps demonstrate how God uses people from various walks of life to serve as prophets. The Lord calls princes as well as paupers, noblemen as well as shepherds. The lesson for us is that He can use every-one of us in His service if we will yield ourselves to His will for our lives.

The prophets Nahum and Habakkuk probably also ministered during the earlier years of the reign of King Josiah of Judah, and Jeremiah soon was called to join them. It was a time of great change and crisis in Judah. Although the Assyrians were about to be overthrown, the armies of Babylon would replace them as a threat to the Hebrew nation.

Some scholars think that Zephaniah was a young man when he gave the messages recorded in this book. One reason for thinking so is that he uses strong and fiery language, which often seems typical of youth. He wanted changes right *now*, if not sooner, as young people often do. Some even call Zephaniah "God's angry young man."

Of course, Zephaniah had good reason for his anger. King Manasseh had been succeeded on the throne by his son Amon, who led the people once again into idolatry. King Josiah was only 8 years old, so it would be a while before he could institute a reform, and when it came it would not last long.

The Day of the Lord

Zephaniah impressively pointed to the coming of the day of the Lord, echoing Joel as he did so. The alarms they both sounded were, and still are, intended to call God's people to repentance, revival, and reforma-tion. Zephaniah, as did Joel, used such hyperbolic or exaggerated terms about what would happen on the day of the Lord that commentators ever since have seen in his words a clear description of the final, universal day of judgment.

God's long-suffering is not to be equated with weakness. The extent and greatness of God's mercy are reflected in the extent and greatness of His wrath in the time of judgment soon to come. If those to whom we are called to give the judgment message are to be awakened to the soon-coming "day of the Lord," it must be now.

In Zephaniah 1:4-6 the prophet listed in descending order the hierarchy of sins for which God's people were to be punished in his day:

1. Baal worship.
2. Idolatrous priests (*Chemarim*).
3. Worship of the sun, moon, and stars.
4. Worship of the true God through created objects.
5. Apostasy, rejection of God.
6. Not seeking the Lord.

Although indifference to God and religion may not be as bad as out-and-out idol worship according to this ranking, the consequences will be the same on the day of the Lord—the day of final judgment.

What Will Be Doom for Some Will Be Deliverance for Others

Verses 14-18 present a vivid description of the day of the Lord. Although Zephaniah at this point dwells on doom and destruction, elsewhere in his book he views the day of judgment from the perspective of the deliverance and delight that it will bring to those who remain faithful to the Lord.

"The final judgment is a most solemn, awful event. This must take place before the universe. To the Lord Jesus the Father has committed all judgment. He will declare the reward of loyalty to all who obey the law of

Jehovah. God will be honored and His government vindicated and glorified, and that in the presence of the inhabitants of the unfallen worlds. . . .

"What a consolation it will be to recognize in the Judge our Teacher and Redeemer, bearing all the marks of the crucifixion, from which shine forth beams of glory, giving additional value to the crowns which the redeemed receive from His hands, the very hands outstretched in blessing over His disciples as He ascended.

"The very voice which said to them, 'Lo, I am with you alway, even unto the end of the world' (Matt. 28:20) bids them welcome to His presence. The very One who gave His precious life for them, who by His grace moved their hearts to repentance, who awakened them to their need of salvation, receives them now into His joy. Oh how they love Him! The realization of their hopes is so much greater than their expectation. They take their glittering crowns and cast them at His feet. Their joy is complete" (Ellen G. White letter 131, 1900 [to A. G. Daniells, Oct. 14, 1900]).

We'll come back to that letter in a moment, but let's look at another letter written some years ago by Dr. Harry Rimmer to Charles Fuller of the Old Fashioned Revival Hour.

"Next Sunday you are to talk about Heaven. I am interested in that land because I have held a clear title to a bit of property over there for more than 50 years. I did not buy it. It was given to me without money and without price; but the donor purchased it for me at a tremendous sacrifice.

"I am not holding it for speculation. It is not a vacant lot. For more than half a century I have been sending materials out of which the greatest Architect of the universe has been building a home for me, which will never need remodeling or repairs because it will suit me perfectly, individually, and will never grow old.

"Termites can never undermine its foundation, for it rests upon the Rock of Ages. Fire cannot destroy it. Floods cannot wash it away. No lock or bolts will ever be placed upon the doors, for no vicious persons can ever enter that land. . . .

"There is a valley of deep shadow between this place where I live, and that to which I shall journey. . . . I cannot reach my home in that city without passing through this valley. But I am not afraid because the best Friend I ever had went through the same valley long ago and drove away all its gloom. He has stuck with me through thick and thin since we first became acquainted 55 years ago, and I hold His promise in printed form never to forsake me or leave me alone. He will be with me as I walk through the valley of the shadow of death, and I shall not lose my way because He is with me" (*The Messenger of Light*, quoted in *Pulpit Helps*, [Chattanooga, Tenn.: AMG International]).

You and I hold a clear title to a piece of property in that land, too. And someday very soon now we will cast our crowns at Jesus' feet as He bids us enter into the city He has prepared for us.

The Price of Acceptance

Jesus paid the price for our property in heaven. But it will cost us something, too. We cannot pay the infinite price of our salvation, but we must pay the price of acceptance. That means that we must be willing to take up the cross and follow Christ's pattern of self-denial and loving obedience to the will of His Father and ours. Going back to Ellen White's letter to Elder A. G. Daniells, we find her adding: "In that great day all will see that their course of action decided their destiny. They will be rewarded or punished according as they have obeyed or violated the law of God. In that great day the character of each individual will be plainly and distinctly revealed. God will look into all the feelings and motives. No one can then occupy middle ground. Men and women are either saints or sinners, either entitled to a glorious life of eternity or doomed to eternal death."

In the light of the coming day of the Lord, the day of final judgment, we need to face seriously the problem of our lack of full commitment to Christ.

Someone has drawn this contrast between our hymns and our hearts:

* We sing "Sweet Hour of Prayer," but are content with just 5 or 10 minutes.

* We sing "Onward, Christian Soldiers!" but wait to be drafted into Christ's service.

* We sing "Showers of Blessing," but do not come to church when it rains.

* We sing "Blest Be the Tie That Binds," but sever our connection with the church as soon as someone offends us.

* We sing "Serve the Lord With Gladness," but gripe if we have to do something for the church.

* We sing "I Love to Tell the Story," but never breathe a word of it to those we contact.

* We sing "I'm but a Stranger Here," but cling to the things of this world as though we had no heaven awaiting us.

* We sing "Wholly Thine," but give so little of ourselves.

* We sing "Faith Is the Victory," but seem to keep giving in to the same old sins over and over again.

In some respects, we are like the boy who stood by an apple barrel in an old-fashioned store with his hand on one of the apples. "Boy, what are you trying to do, steal my apples?" the storekeeper challenged.

"No, sir, I'm not," the boy said. "I'm trying hard not to steal one."

We need to take our hand away from the apple barrel and put it in the hand of Christ.

Josiah's Revival

King Josiah was just a boy of 8 when he began to rule Judah during the time of Zephaniah. But he determined not to put his hand in the apple barrel. The Bible tells us, "Like unto him was there no king before him, that turned to the Lord with all his heart, and with all his soul, and with all his might, according to all the law of Moses; neither after him arose there any like him" (2 Kings 23:25).

Josiah's grandfather was wicked Manasseh, who, after a long life of wickedness finally turned to the Lord in his old age. The young king's father was even worse. Amon was one of the most wicked of all the wicked kings of Judah. But in vivid contrast to this evil stands the boy-king, Josiah.

Perhaps one of the reasons God sent the young man Zephaniah as a prophet to Judah during Josiah's reign was that the Lord wanted to encourage the king to bring about a great revival and reformation. Remarkably, God predicted Josiah's reform, mentioning him by name 300 years before he was born. A prophet was sent to tell King Jeroboam, who was at that moment engaged in defying God by officiating as a priest at the new altar in Bethel, that "a child shall be born unto the house of David, Josiah by name" (1 Kings 13:2). He was to burn the bones of the pagan priests at that very site.

Josiah's task was formidable. As the first part of the book of Zephaniah indicates, idolatry was being practiced everywhere. The heavenly bodies were worshiped openly at the royal court. The Temple copy of the book of the law had become lost through "careless neglect" (*Prophets and Kings*, p. 393).

But the "silent yet powerful influences set in operation by the messages of the prophets . . . did much to prepare the way for the reformation that took place in the eighteenth year of Josiah's reign. This reform movement, by which threatened judgments were averted for a season, was brought about in a wholly unexpected manner through the discovery and study of a portion of Holy Scripture that for many years had been strangely misplaced and lost" (*ibid.*, p. 392).

As the earnest young king began the repair of the Temple, God blessed him by allowing the scrolls of the book of the law to be recovered by Hilkiah the priest. Josiah was deeply stirred as he listened for the first time to the words written by Moses under the inspiration of the Holy Spirit. While Shaphan the scribe read the words of the scroll to him, the king "discerned in this volume a treasure of knowledge, a powerful ally, in the work of reform he so much desired to see wrought in the land. He resolved to walk in the light of its counsels, and also to do all in his power to acquaint his people with its teachings and to lead them, if possible, to cultivate reverence and love for the law of heaven" (*ibid.*, p. 398).

It is interesting to Adventists today that when the king wanted to understand better how to use the newly recovered book of the law to bring about a revival and reformation and to save his nation if possible, he turned to the prophetess Huldah for guidance. Through her God revealed that the people were so hardened in their sins that the threatened punishment of captivity in Babylon would have to take place in the future, but it could be averted for a time by a work of genuine repentance and reformation. Josiah proceeded to do all he could to destroy idolatry and bring about a new national commitment to the Lord.

Josiah and his people went to work with a new commitment to restore the worship of the true God.

Here we find a clue to the best way to deal with sin. Replace evil with good. Go to work for God. Put His work and interests first. Then you will be too busy to sin. Better than our attempts to eradicate sin by fighting it is getting so busy in God's work of reform that we have no time to devote to sin.

One activity that was foremost in crowding out sin was the people's effort to take time to study and appreciate God's Word. They turned their complete attention to the law and to the testimonies to find out what God wanted them to do.

Whatever God wanted done, Josiah wanted done. He turned neither to the right nor to the left. He chose to do God's will as a boy and pursued that commitment every day of his life. The text used to begin this section reveals the secret of his success: "And like unto him was there no king before him, that turned to the Lord with all his heart, and with all his soul, and with all his might" (2 Kings 23:25).

Will we turn to the Lord with all our might now in the time of earth's last great crisis? Will we be revived by a new commitment to the study of the law and the testimonies that will crowd out sin in our lives? These are serious times. This *is* the day of the Lord that Joel and Zephaniah predicted would bring in the dawn of eternity. God challenges through His prophet, "Gather together, gather together, O shameful nation, before the appointed time arrives and that day sweeps on like chaff, before the fierce anger of the Lord comes upon you, before the day of the Lord's wrath comes upon you. Seek the Lord, all you humble of the land, you who do what he commands. Seek righteousness, seek humility; perhaps you will be sheltered on the day of the Lord's anger" (Zeph. 2:1-3, NIV). If we are not ready for the day of the Lord, we must face the fierce wrath of God poured out without mercy in the final judgment.

Does God Send Judgments?

In volume 8 of the *Testimonies*, Ellen White published a letter that she read to the Review and Herald board in November 1901. In it she warned, "I feel a terror of soul as I see to what a pass our publishing house has come. The presses in the Lord's institution have been printing the soul-destroying theories of Romanism and other mysteries of iniquity. The office must be purged of this objectionable matter" (p. 91).

This was read more than two years before the fire that destroyed the publishing house in Battle Creek. Ellen White added the following warning: "Those who show by their actions that they make no effort to distinguish between the sacred and the common may know that, unless they repent, God's judgments will fall on them. These judgments may be delayed, but they will come" (p. 95).

Perhaps a brief aside at this point is necessary. Ellen White was referring to the commercial printing work that the publishing houses had begun doing. However, she did not view commercial printing within the publishing houses as all bad. Earlier she had encouraged the houses to engage in commercial printing because it was "one of the means by which these [publishing] institutions are brought in contact with the world," thus opening "a door . . . for the communication of the light of truth" (*ibid.*, vol. 7, p. 161).

But she specifically mentions several serious problems that the acceptance of commercial work was causing or might cause. Despite these potential problems, Ellen White was still able to say: "It is not necessary that the commercial work should be entirely divorced from the publishing houses" (7T, p. 163). So it was not commercial work in and of itself that she was condemning but a misuse that endangered the very mission of the publishing work of the church.

But back to our main issue: Does God Himself send judgments? After the fire at the publishing house, Elder L. McCoy, a member of the Board of Directors for a number of years, declared: "I have no sympathy with the idea that the burning of the Review and Herald was a judgment from God. That is heathenism. The heathen, whenever they have any calamity or pestilence, think their god is angry with them, and they go to work to do something to appease his anger. They have no such thing in their theology or religion as tenderness, love, mercy, and forgiveness."

Ellen White did not agree. In a letter written on January 5, 1903, from St. Helena, California, she stated: "Today I received a letter from Elder Daniells regarding the destruction of the Review office by fire. . . . I was not surprised by the sad news, for in the visions of the night I have seen an angel standing with a sword of fire stretched over Battle Creek. Once, in the daytime, while my pen was in my hand, I lost consciousness, and it seemed as if this sword of flame were turning first in one direction and then in another. Disaster seemed to follow disaster, because God was dishonored by the devising of men to exalt and glorify themselves. . . .

"Men may erect the most carefully constructed, fireproof buildings, but one touch of God's hand, one spark from heaven, will sweep away every refuge" (*Testimonies*, vol. 8, pp. 97-99).

What some do not understand is that God's law is our protection and shelter from His wrath poured out in the seven last plagues. The ninety-first psalm teaches us that no harm will befall those who dwell in the shelter of the Most High, neither will any plague come nigh their dwelling.

Because of our Laodicean apathy, God still must apply the shock treatment to His people, as He did back in Zephaniah's day. What He wants to do is help the scales fall from our eyes in order that we might see His love in His standard of righteousness—that we might recognize His law as our covering and protection. When we do, then we will be so enamored of God's will and become so busy in His service that sin will be crowded out of our lives.

CHAPTER
11

"Seek Ye the Lord"

Chapter 1 of Zephaniah closes on a note of solemn warning. The trumpet of judgment is sounding, and the people are not prepared for what is to come. Is there no hope? The first three verses of chapter 2 declare that there *is* hope for both ancient and modern Israel. But that hope depends on God's people responding to His appeal to turn to Him in full commitment to His plan for them and for the restoration of eternal peace in the world. The proud and stubborn are to seek His meekness and righteousness as the only means of escape from the punishment that has been pronounced on those refusing to heed God's appeal.

Call to Repentance

God's call to "gather together" and repent is addressed to the "shameful nation" (Zeph. 2:1, NIV) of Judah. After the "decree" that composes most of chapter 1 would go into effect, it would be too late to change the fate of the nation. The "chaff" would be scattered as before a whirlwind. The Lord was about to withdraw Himself from His professed people, allowing the Babylonians to invade and take them captive. The "day of the Lord" was about to occur. If ever there was a time for heart-searching, prayer, and unity of spirit, that was the time.

We live in an even more crucial time when the final "day of the Lord" is soon to take place. After quoting Zephaniah 2:1-3, Ellen White drives the lesson home forcefully: "We are near the close of time. . . . In infinite mercy a last warning message has been sent to the world, announcing that Christ is at the door. . . . The day is just upon us when the righteous shall be bound like precious grain in bundles for the heavenly garner, while the wicked are, like the tares, gathered for the fires of the last great day. . . . Those who are drinking from the same fountain of blessing will draw nearer together. Truth dwelling in the hearts of believers will lead to blessed and happy assimilation. Thus will be answered the prayer of Christ that His disciples might be one even as he is one with the Father. For this oneness every truly converted heart will be striving" (*Testimonies*, vol. 5, pp. 99-101).

The real thrust of these first few verses of chapter 2 probably can be visualized best in chart form as follows:

Zephaniah 2:1-3—God's Appeal	
1, 2	**3a**
"Gather together" before 1. the decree takes effect 2. the day passes as the chaff 3. the fierce anger of the Lord comes on you	1. "Seek ye the Lord" 2. "Seek righteousness" 3. "Seek meekness"
3b—God's Promise—"It may be ye shall be hid in the day of the Lord's anger."	

The Call to Unity

In Ephesians 4:3, Paul challenges the church to "make every effort to keep the unity of the Spirit through the bond of peace" (NIV). The apostle, of course, was well acquainted with the church he had raised up at Ephesus. He knew firsthand about their first-love experience. In presenting the challenge found in this verse, he assumed that the experience of oneness still characterized the believers in the Ephesian church and urged them to maintain that oneness and unity. Nothing gives so much grace and character to a church as being able to observe love and oneness among its members.

In the verses that follow, Paul proceeded to outline seven particulars in which unity and oneness should be manifested in God's church. He lists:

1. *One body*—Christians belong to the family of God.

2. *One Spirit*—All the gifts and graces in Christian life come from the Holy Spirit.

3. *One hope*—The blessed hope of Christ's soon return.

4. *One Lord*—Who loves us and is the supreme object of our loyalty.

5. *One faith*—Through accepting the salvation provided by Jesus.

6. *One baptism*—The outward symbol of our union with Christ.

7. *One God and Father of us all*—The source of our unity and oneness. As God is one, we are to be one.

Yet in unity and oneness, the church still is made up of individuals. In the next several verses, Paul indicates that when Christ ascended on high He gave gifts to His church—the gifts of the Spirit. He did not give the same gifts to everyone, but gave different talents, gifts, and a particular work to each one of us. No one is without a gift, but none shares exactly the same gifts in the same way. There is a diversity in gifts and perceptions, yet we are to find unity in our diversity.

He distributed these gifts to build up the body of Christ, not to tear it down. They will be manifested in the church until the experience portrayed in verses 13-16 has been achieved: "So shall we at last attain to the unity inherent in our faith and our knowledge of the Son of God—to mature manhood, measured by nothing less than the full stature of Christ. We are no longer to be children, tossed by the waves and whirled about by every fresh gust of teaching, dupes of crafty rogues and their deceitful schemes. No, let us speak the truth in love; so shall we fully grow up into Christ. He is the head, and on him the whole body depends. Bonded and knit together by every constituent joint, the whole frame grows through the due activity of each part, and builds itself up in love" (NEB). What a beautiful portrait of what God makes possible for His church!

Paul also challenges us to present to the world an authentic vision of the glory of God in the face of Christ by letting Him be seen in us (see 2 Cor. 4:6).

One day as Leonardo da Vinci was working on his masterpiece, *The Last Supper*, he became angry at one of his acquaintances. He lashed out at him with bitter words. Then he returned to his work on the face of Christ. But he was unable to paint that patient face while there was bitterness in his heart. The artist stopped painting and went looking for the man who was the object of his anger. On finding him, he begged his forgiveness. Only after Da Vinci had made things right could he go back and complete the face of Christ. We too must make the wrongs we have committed right before we can adequately portray the love of Christ to the world.

Collectively, we must "gather together" in love and unity in order to complete the work God has given us to do on earth.

The Meek Called to "Seek"

In Zephaniah 2:3 the Lord turns from the "shameless" (RSV) in Judah who have no sense of guilt for their sins to address the "meek," those who are humble and responsive. Their characters stand in sharp contrast to the proud and self-sufficient, who are too busy with themselves to pay attention to the warnings God has given.

The New International Version translates the word that the King James translators rendered as "meek" as follows: "You who do what he commands."

That fits Ellen White's comment: "Here is our work. It is not sinners who are here addressed, but all the meek of the earth, who have wrought His judgments or kept His commandments" (*Testimonies*, vol. 1, p. 426).

What Three Steps Are "the Meek" to Take?

1. "Seek ye the Lord"—Seeking involves our search to learn who God is and what He has in mind concerning the way we should live.

The Bible passages that follow help us understand better what it means to seek the Lord and why it is essential to do so: Deuteronomy 4:29 tells us that if we seek the Lord "with all thy heart and with all thy soul," we shall find Him. Amos 5:4 promises that if we seek the Lord we shall live. Colossians 3:1 urges those who have "risen with Christ" to "seek those things which are above." Hebrews 11:6 assures us that God "is a rewarder of them that diligently seek him."

A fascinating aspect of "seeking" is found in Ezekiel 34:11, 12 and Luke 19:10. God is said to be seeking us. In other words, His challenge is, Seek Me until I find you.

2. "Seek righteousness"—Righteousness not only involves right-being but also right-doing. If we have His love in our hearts, we will keep His law. In the first table of the law, we see that "if man love God in all the breadth and beauty suggested by the words 'with all thy heart, and with all thy soul, and with all thy mind,' he cannot possibly find room for another God, and so the first word is kept. If man love God supremely, he will not suffer anything to stand between him and God, thus the graven image is broken to pieces, and swept away by the force of a stronger affection. Out of love will spring that hallowing of the name of God which will dry the springs of blasphemy, and make the double dealing of the hypocrite an impossibility. The Sabbath will be eagerly welcomed, and all its privileges earnestly and gladly appropriated when it is a season in which love may find its way into the attitude of worship, and the acts of service flowing therefrom.

"Passing to the second table, and looking now at love in its working toward others, it will at once be seen that the only sufficient power for obedience and honor rendered to parents is that of love. There will be no thought of murder until the awful moment has arrived in which the flame of love has died out upon the altar. Unchastity of every description is love's sure destruction, growing gross upon the very death of that which it so vilely personates. All theft is rendered impossible by true love for one's neighbor. Love sits as a sentinel at the portal of the lips, and arrests the faintest whisper of false witness against a neighbor; nay, rather dwells within the heart, and slays the thought that might have inspired the whisper. It is love and love alone that, finding satisfaction in God, satisfies the heart's hunger, and prevents all coveting" (G. Campbell Morgan, *The Ten Commandments* [New York: Fleming H. Revell Company, 1901], pp. 120, 121).

Righteousness not only applies to God's cleansing our past sins; its work also involves what He does to keep us from falling into sin. "Sanctification is a state of holiness, without and within, being holy and without reserve the Lord's, not in form, but in truth. Every impurity of thought, every lustful passion, separates the soul from God; for Christ can never put His robe of righteousness upon a sinner, to hide his deformity. . . . There must be a progressive work of triumph over evil, of sympathy with good, a reflection of the character of Jesus" (*Our High Calling*, p. 214).

3. *"Seek meekness"*—Meekness is not cowardice. In fact it is just the opposite because it involves full submission to the will of God. That is not easy for human beings. Actually, it is impossible unless the grace of God makes it possible for us to so submit ourselves fully to Him.

When we are willing to humble ourselves, to empty ourselves in order to be vessels to hold the mercies of God, the Lord will be able to use us. He will fill us full of blessings to bestow on those about us.

"Ye Shall Be Hid"

In chapter 4 of this book we touched on the promise that God would shelter His people during the time of the outpouring of His wrath on deserving sinners. There it was stated that the promise of Zephaniah 2:3 can be applied primarily to God's protection of His people during the seven last plagues. The verses listed below from Psalm 91 bring us the following assurances:

1. We will abide under the shadow of the Almighty.
2. He will be our refuge and fortress.
3. He will deliver us.
4. He will cover us.
5. We will not be afraid.
7. Death will be all around us but shall not come on us.
8. We will see the reward of wicked but will not receive it.

10. No evil or plague will harm us.

11, 12. Angels will protect us.

14-16. God gives us His personal promise.

Note who is protected, according to the psalm: those who dwell in God's secret place; those who belong to the Lord; those who have made the Lord their refuge and habitation; those whom God has surrounded with His love, who know Him, and who call on Him.

"In that day [the time of the seven last plagues], multitudes will desire the shelter of God's mercy which they have so long despised. . . .

"The people of God will not be free from suffering; but while persecuted and distressed, while they endure privation and suffer for want of food they will not be left to perish. . . . He who numbers the hairs of their heads will care for them. . . . While the wicked are dying from hunger and pestilence, angels will shield the righteous and supply their wants."

"If the blood of Christ's faithful witnesses were shed at this time, it would not, like the blood of the martyrs, be as seed sown to yield a harvest for God. . . . If the righteous were now left to fall a prey to their enemies, it would be a triumph for the prince of darkness" (*The Great Controversy*, pp. 629, 634; see also Isa. 26:20, 21).

If we meet the conditions outlined in the first part of Zephaniah 2:3, there is no question but that God will hide us from the destruction that comes upon the world "in the day of the Lord's anger." What a truly blessed hope is ours!

CHAPTER 10

12

"After This the Judgment"

To the amusement of his new congregation, a young minister was confronted by the village skeptic, Burt Olney, at the close of his first service. Olney challenged the pastor by saying, "You did well. But I don't believe that the Bible is infallible."

In response, the young minister calmly asserted, " 'It is appointed unto men once to die, but after this the judgment' " (Heb. 9:27).

"Well, I can prove that there is no such thing as judgment after death," Olney declared.

"But men do die," the minister replied. " 'For it is appointed unto men once to die, but after this the judgment.' "

"That's no argument," the skeptic huffed. "Let's get down to business and discuss this matter properly."

Shaking his head, the young minister answered, "I'm not here to argue. My business is to preach the Word of God."

Olney was disappointed and angry. "I don't believe you know enough about the Bible to be able to argue about it," he responded.

"Perhaps you're right," the minister answered. "But

'It is appointed unto men once to die, but after this the judgment.' "

Olney walked away toward home. But the very tree toads seemed to be repeating that verse. As he crossed a little stream, it seemed that the frogs joined in the chorus, " 'It is appointed unto men once to die, but after this the judgment.' " That night as Burt tried to sleep, all that he could think of was "judgment, judgment, judgment!"

Early the next morning Burt Olney appeared at the pastor's door. "I have come to see you about the text you gave me yesterday. Those words keep burning into my soul. Tell me, what do I have to do to be ready to meet God in the judgment?"

When Olney left the minister later that day, he had become a child of God who, through the grace of Christ, could look forward boldly to the time of judgment.

Who's Afraid of the Judgment?

God warns us of the inevitability of judgment not only to help us realize the nature and results of sin, but to enable us to "have boldness in the day of judgment; because as he [the Son of God] is, so are we in this world" (1 John 4:17).

How do you personally feel about the judgment that will surely come? The Christian, committed and secure in forgiveness and acceptance, has no reason for concern. George Vandeman likens it to traveling on a train. As the cars lurch along, each passenger is busy with his or her own thoughts or pastime. Suddenly the door at one end of a coach opens, and the conductor's loud voice demands, "Tickets!" Suppose you are there, and tucked safely into your pocket is your ticket—your right to travel on the train (in this case, glory bound). As the conductor approaches your seat, does panic rise in your throat? Does your heart pound? Of course not. *You have a ticket.* Terror is only for those who do not have one.

As is true of most of the minor prophets, Zephaniah has a lot to say about the judgment. The section we are focusing on in this chapter can be outlined as in the chart that follows:

Zephaniah 2:4-3:7—The Lessons of Judgment	
2:4-3:4—Judgments	**3:5-7—Lessons**
The List of Those Judged: 2:4-7—Philistia 2:8-11—Moab and Ammon 2:12—Ethiopia 2:13-15—Assyria 3:1-5—Judah	3:5—The people's sins contrasted with God's righteousness 3:6, 7—God's amazement at Judah's inability to learn from others

Why does God spend so much time and so many words in warning about the great judgment day? It seems that He cannot let anyone go without an outpouring of concern from His great heart of love in that individual's behalf. The judgment is coming, but we can be ready. Anyone who wants a ticket can have one.

Judgment on the Persecutors

Some commentators view this section of Zephaniah as a threat to Judah. Just as surely as the other nations are to be judged, the people of Judah will be punished for their sins. Other writers consider it as a message of comfort, pointing out that Judah's persecutors to the west, east, south, and north are to be punished for what they have done to God's people. Undoubtedly, both elements enter into what God intended the prophet to convey.

The fertile land of Philistia lay to the west of Palestine. Zephaniah mentioned four of its important cities as being ripe for judgment. The fifth, Gath, had apparently already been destroyed by the Assyrians. Goliath was a citizen of this city, and he can be considered typical of the "sea people's" brutal attitude toward their eastern neighbors. Reports of savage attacks on God's people by the Philistines are scattered throughout the early books of the Bible.

When this prophecy was given, the cities of Gaza, Ashkelon, Ashdod, and Ekron were about to face the Judge. Zephaniah speaks of Ashdod being driven out "at the noon day," indicating an unexpected and sudden destruction.

Records of the Assyrians show that their armies invaded and subjugated the Philistines. Later most of the Philistine territory became part of Herod's kingdom.

Verse 7 could be a great comfort to the beleaguered citizens of Judah. The whole coast would be theirs. They would eat and relax in the houses of their former enemies, and best of all, the Lord Himself would visit them, and they would never again be captives.

So we, the modern children of God, committed and mature in Jesus Christ, may joyously rest from our personal enemies—pride and self-seeking. God will visit us because He delights to be with us, and we shall be free in Him forever.

Judgment on Lot's Children

To the east of Palestine lived the children of Lot and his daughters—the Moabites and Ammonites. Isaiah mentions pride as their besetting sin (see Isa. 16:6). These bitter enemies have reviled and reproached God's people, while promoting themselves. Now they are to be as abandoned as Sodom and Gomorrah.

The *Pulpit Commentary* gives this eyewitness account of Moab at the time the commentary was written: "All is desolate. Not a building, and scarcely a fragment of a wall, is standing; yet, though deserted for centuries, it bears its ancient name. I looked from Heshbon far and wide over the ancient territory of the Moabites, and saw desolation everywhere. The old towns and villages are all deserted and in ruins. In fact, there is not at this moment a single inhabited town or village in Moab, except Kerak, which stands on the extreme southern border. . . . The cities, towns, villages, are all in ruins. . . . And no attempt is ever made to rebuild or repair; no man ventures to seek even a temporary abode among the ruined cities of Moab. The local Arab avoids the old sites, and seeks rest and security amid rocks and ravines; the powerful desert tribes sweep over the country periodically, and devour and destroy all in their track" (vol. 32, p. 28).

The chilling statement of Zephaniah 2:11, "The Lord will be terrible unto them," demonstrates that a sad end is the inevitable result of sin. But that sad end is essential in order for the next, thrilling, part of verse 11 to take place: "And men shall worship him [God], every one from his place."

Hope for the Rich?

Ethiopia lay to the south of Palestine; partly in what is now Egypt and partly in the Sudan. When the Bible speaks of "my sword," it refers to the instrument of God's punishment, whatever that instrument may be. The prophecy will have its finest and purest fulfillment when these words come to pass: "Princes shall come out of Egypt: Ethiopia shall soon stretch out her hands unto God" (Ps. 68:31).

In the time of Zephaniah, Egypt and Ethiopia were rich, and may be considered as representing the time when wealthy and powerful nations will turn at last to the God of us all.

Judgment in the North

From the deep south the prophet turns to the far north, where Assyria still flourished. Again, pride is a besetting sin. At this time Assyria maintained a remarkable system of irrigation. When the citizens were unable to keep this in working order, the artificially lush countryside soon relapsed into an arid desert. The "flocks" and "herds" of Zephaniah 2:14 do not refer to docile groups of domestic sheep and goats but, instead, to the wild animals that roamed the land.

Picture if you can the beasts slinking about, the mournful hooting of owls mingled with the strident cawing of crows, and the houses in a sad state of disrepair. Then turn your attention to verse 15: "That is what will happen to the city that is so proud of its own power and thinks it is safe" (TEV).

God Is Always Just

God would contradict His own system of justice if He were to overlook that His people were committing the same kind of sins. It would not be right for Him to punish the heathen and let His chosen people go free. Listen to the list of Judah's transgressions. They are indistinguishable from those of the idolaters around them:

3:1—Jerusalem is corrupt and rebellious. It oppresses its own people.

3:2—The people of the city do not listen to the Lord nor accept His discipline. They do not trust Him or ask for His help.

3:3—The leaders are like animals as they prey on the citizens.

3:4—The religious leaders are irresponsible and treacherous. They defile what is sacred.

Despite this disheartening picture, there is hope.

God has not changed at all. He still remains among His people, saddened to be sure, but He does not let this hinder Him from doing what is right. The unjust will have reason to be ashamed, but God's faithful few will rejoice in Him.

Verse 7 gives an explanation as to why God has been fierce in His punishment of the wicked. He had hoped to redeem them unto Himself. How crushing their failure must have been to the divine heart! In agony He cries out, "I punished them: but they rose early, and corrupted all their doings."

How About Us?

But what does this mean to us? Do you see yourself in any of the actions or reactions recounted in Zephaniah? Do you feel at times that God has singled you out for punishment, and you don't like it at all?

Remember, it is only in love that He chastens us, only to revive and prepare us for eternity. If we were not worth something, He would not take time to work with us. "Thou shalt also consider in thine heart, that, as a man chasteneth his son, so the Lord thy God chasteneth thee. Therefore thou shalt keep the commandments of the Lord thy God, to walk in his ways, and to fear him" (Deut. 8:5, 6).

The records of God's dealing with the nations and His people in the past teach us a precious lesson. The Lord will do everything possible to save us and to make sure that we will have His love in our hearts so that we can face the coming judgment with holy boldness. But He cannot and will not force us to accept Him and be ready for the judgment. We are deciding right now whether or not we will accept the ticket that entitles us to be on the train bound for heaven. After this comes the judgment.

13

When God Sings

Judgment need not be considered a time of doom and gloom. For those whom God delivers from the tyranny of sin, it is a day of rejoicing. In fact, God Himself will rejoice over the outcome of judgment. Zephaniah pictures Him singing a happy song about the results (see Zeph. 3:17). If faithful, we will be there to hear the greatest solo ever sung. Imagine, if you can, what a spectacular and impressive singing voice the Creator of Lucifer must have. Lucifer's voice was so wonderful that he "led the heavenly choir." He was the one who "raised the first note" (*The Story of Redemption*, p. 25). His voice must have had the range and tone of the greatest of pipe organs. But how much sweeter and melodious must be the voice of God!

What will God have to sing about? Will He be singing about the destruction of the wicked? Of course not. God does not enjoy destroying His wicked children any more than those of us who will witness the destruction of many we have loved will enjoy that essential but sorrow-packed moment of time. But the *results* of the final judgment will thrill God's heart and the hearts of every being in the universe. Sin, sorrow, death, misery, disease, and crime will be no more. Judgment will be infinitely painful to the loving heart of God, but He will be willing to suffer that agony, as He knows that it will be the final act of suffering for the rest of eternity.

Notice in the chart that follows how this last section of Zephaniah's book points forward to the time when we will be home at last.

Zephaniah 3:8-20—The Result of Judgment		
8-13	14-17	18-20
Restoration after punishment	God and His people rejoice	God's people return home

The original, limited application of these verses probably refers to the punishment of Israel and other nations near them by the Babylonians and the subsequent restoration of a remnant of God's people. But the universality of this description and of the restored state of the remnant who return indicate a larger application—an ultimate restoration of the people of God at Christ's second coming and the final judgment at the end of the millennium.

God Is in Control

One of the most often asked questions on the part of Bible writers was "Why do the wicked seem to prosper and the righteous have so many difficulties?"

Job had that problem until God revealed to him that He was in charge and knew what He was doing. David raised the same question in Psalm 37, as did the psalmist Asaph in the seventy-third psalm. Both found their answer when they went into the sanctuary and realized that God was in control and that the ultimate answer could be found in the final rewards handed out at the time of the judgment.

But Habakkuk received the clearest answer of all to

this universal question. God's message to him was in essence: "Don't worry about that, Habakkuk. I'm aware of what it must seem like to you. But I'm already taking care of that problem. Inherent in evil is its own destruction. Although the wicked seem to prosper, they do not find happiness in what they achieve through selfishness and greed. But, more than that, I'm sitting in judgment in My holy temple, and all wrongs will be made right on the final day of judgment. I know all about what is going on. I am in control. I am the final judge. Eventually My justice will be evident when the entire universe will stand in awestricken silence before My throne."

Habakkuk was told that God's purposes know no delay (see Hab. 2:3). When the clock of probationary time has run down, it will be seen that righteousness and justice will prevail after all. Sin and its terrible consequences will be eliminated from God's perfect universe forever. Then the singing will break out—glorious, happy, thrilling singing such as has never been heard before in all the universe. And God Himself will lead out in that triumphant song.

The Song of the Redeemed

After God has destroyed the sin-degraded earth by fire (see Zeph. 3:8), He is pictured as giving His people a "pure language" (verse 9). "No matter from what nation or tongue they might be, all those who join Israel in worshiping the true God will speak a 'pure language,' no longer polluted by idolatry in any of its forms (see Ps. 16:4; Hosea 2:17)" (*The Seventh-day Adventist Bible Commentary*, vol. 4, p. 1068). Those whom God has delivered will use that new, pure language to call in unison upon the name of the Lord. As they do so, they will lift their voices in praise and thanksgiving (see Zeph. 3:14).

Ellen White presents this picture of that glorious scene: "As Jesus opens before them [the redeemed] the riches of redemption and the amazing achievements in the great controversy with Satan, the hearts of the ransomed thrill with more fervent devotion, and with more rapturous joy they sweep the harps of gold; and ten thousand times ten thousand and thousands of thousands of voices unite to swell the mighty chorus of praise" (*The Great Controversy*, p. 678).

John the Revelator tells us what the words of that victory song will be: "And every creature which is in heaven, and on the earth, and under the earth, and such as are in the sea, and all that are in them, heard I saying, Blessing, and honour, and glory, and power, be unto him that sitteth upon the throne, and unto the Lamb for ever and ever" (Rev. 5:13).

All creation joins in that song. Isaiah pictures even inanimate creation singing: "The wilderness and the solitary place shall be glad for them; and the desert shall rejoice, and blossom as the rose. It shall blossom abundantly, and rejoice even with joy and singing" (Isa. 35:1, 2).

He adds that "then shall the lame man leap as an hart, and the tongue of the dumb sing" (verse 6).

Isaiah's portrayal of the happy, thrilling song of eternity concludes with these words: "And the ransomed of the Lord shall return, and come to Zion with songs and everlasting joy upon their heads: they shall obtain joy and gladness, and sorrow and sighing shall flee away" (verse 10).

Oh, what a glorious anthem of praise will fill the universe when we are home at last! Then God "will joy over" us "with singing" (Zeph. 3:17).

Home at Last

The last part of Zephaniah 3:13 reads: "For they shall feed and lie down, and none shall make them afraid." There is a close parallel here to what Psalm 23 portrays happening under the ministry of the Lord our shepherd. When we belong to God fully, nothing can harm us or make us afraid.

Zephaniah reacts to this tremendous promise with the challenge "Sing, O daughter of Zion; shout, O Israel: be glad and rejoice with all the heart, O daughter of Jerusalem" (verse 14). We cannot sing now as we will in heaven, but when we realize all that God is doing and will do for our salvation, we can shout out His praise with voices that do not yet match what they will be when lifted in praise in the earth made new.

The last words of Zephaniah's prophecy form a clear, ringing call to us to enter into a much-needed revival today that will lead us into the Promised Land: "At that time I will gather you; at that time I will bring you home" (verse 20, NIV).

Should not such thrilling promises as those we find in the last chapter of Zephaniah lead us to an intense longing for our heavenly home?

Ellen White was shown heaven in vision. Notice how she expressed her longing for her eternal home: "If we can meet Jesus in peace and be saved, forever saved, we shall be the happiest of beings! Oh, to be at home at last where the wicked cease from troubling and the weary are at rest! Heaven, sweet heaven! Oh, I shall appreciate heaven! I know that I must watch and keep my garments unspotted from the world or I shall never enter the abode of the blessed. The east is not separated farther from the west than the children of light are separated from the children of darkness. We must watch continually and pray always that we may not be overcome with Satan's devices. I long for a greater faith, a more earnest consecration" (letter 113, 1886).

Do we have the same longing?

Dr. Clarence Macartney is best known for his sermon "Come Before Winter." He first presented it in the Arch

Street Presbyterian Church in Philadelphia in 1915. Every October from that time on he preached this same sermon until he preached it for the last time in 1945 in the First Presbyterian Church in Pittsburgh, where he had served as pastor since 1926.

The sermon is based on the words Paul wrote from his prison in Rome. Paul urged his young friend, Timothy, to come to Rome to assist him, and to come before winter (see 2 Tim. 4:21).

Reaction to Dr. Macartney's "Come Before Winter" sermon often came to him by mail. Here is one sample from the file he kept: "Your sermon tonight fell like a bombshell. Never has anything so soul-rending struck me. I must act quickly before the steel is cold. Winter has already closed in some opportunities over the past years, but you have given me my greatest opportunity tonight. Five years to date, if I have proved myself to have changed the course of my existence from this night on, I will send you my signature. This is written tonight in deep appreciation of a powerful message, the sort that may shape the course of a young man's life."

I have no way of knowing whether or not Dr. Macartney received that letter five years later or not. But his sermon, repeated each October for 31 years, blessed thousands. Read for a moment the words of the unforgettable conclusion of that sermon that touched so many hearts: "Once again, I repeat these words of the apostle, 'Come before winter;' and as I pronounce them, common sense, experience, conscience, Scripture, the Holy Spirit, . . . and the Lord Jesus Christ all repeat with me, 'Come before winter.' Come before the haze of Indian summer has faded from the fields; come before the November winds strip the leaves from the trees and send them whirling over the fields; come before the snows lie on the uplands and the meadow brook is turned to ice; come before the heart is cold; come before desire has failed; come before life is over and your probation ended and you stand before God to give account of the use you have made of the opportunities which in His grace He has granted. Come before winter! Come to thy God in time."

Those words from the past echo in our hearts today along with Jesus' gracious invitation to get ready for His coming. "And the Spirit and the bride say, Come. And let him that heareth say, Come. And let him that is athirst come. And whosoever will, let him take the water of life freely" (Rev. 22:17).

The messages of the prophets Joel, Micah, and Zephaniah call us to revival now. It is the greatest and most urgent of all our needs. It will prepare the way for the finishing of the Lord's work on earth and the coming of Jesus. If we truly want Jesus to come, what are we waiting for? All heaven, all the universe, is waiting eagerly for us to take to heart the promises we have been studying and to begin to take the practical steps that only we can take to bring about revival—renewed and intense Bible study, confession, repentance, humiliation of heart and life, a genuine interest in the salvation of others, but, most of all, deep, meaningful, earnest prayer that claims God's promises for personal spiritual growth and for the outpouring of His Holy Spirit in latter rain power.

If we commit ourselves unreservedly to His purpose for our lives, we will have revival now and soon will enjoy the thrilling privilege of listening to God Himself sing the great song of rejoicing over a redeemed universe.

BIBLE BOOKSHELF
Inspirational books that bring a richer blessing to your Bible study

Blessed Assurance, by William Johnsson. Habakkuk and Hebrews both speak to Christians today in a manner that is often startling. Paper, 144 pages. US$6.95, Cdn$8.70.

From Rebellion to Restoration, by Arnold Wallenkampf. Explores Ezekiel's message of restoration to God's people who were discouraged by defeat and exile, a message that inspires God's people today as they wait for release from the captivity of this sinful world. Paper, 110 pages. US$7.95, Cdn$9.95.

The God Who Says Yes, by Walter Scragg. In the book of Luke we see a God and a Saviour who accepted everybody: publicans, women, and others whom society looked down on. Paper, 128 pages. US$6.95, Cdn$8.70.

God's Church in a Hostile World, by Joseph Battistone. The author draws on Old Testament passages to help us understand John's visions as recorded in the book of Revelation. Paper, 140 pages. US$7.95, Cdn$9.95.

God's Solution to Man's Dilemma, by Herbert Kiesler. The author explores the theme of righteousness by faith that undergirds the book of Romans. Paper, 128 pages. US$7.95, Cdn$9.95.

The In-between God, by Walter Scragg. In this study on Acts, the Holy Spirit is portrayed as the "In-between God," the one who mediates, enables, and persuades. Paper, 128 pages. US$6.95, Cdn$8.70.

Love Come Home, by Robert Pierson. Using the books Hosea and Philemon, the author explores how God's people should respond to His great love for them today. Paper, 125 pages. US$6.95, Cdn$8.70.

Never Far From Grace, by Rosalie Haffner Lee. The books of 1 and 2 Samuel present God's people making choices that would shape their destiny. But no matter how poor the decision, they were never far from God's grace. Paper, 128 pages. US$7.95, Cdn$9.95.

Portraits of the Messiah in Zechariah, by Philip Samaan. Each chapter focuses on a different aspect of Christ's character and ministry. Paper, 128 pages. US$7.95, Cdn$9.95.

Call or write your Adventist Book Center to order, or write to: ABC Mailing Service, P.O. Box 1119, Hagerstown, MD 21741. Send check or money order. Enclose applicable sales tax and 15 percent (minimum US$2.50) for postage and handling. Prices and availability subject to change without notice.

Call Your ABC Toll-free
1-800-765-6955

Expand your understanding
of the Bible
with *The SDA Bible Commentary*

This 10-volume set includes seven volumes of verse-by-verse commentary and the *SDA Bible Dictionary*, *SDA Bible Students' Source Book*, and *SDA Encyclopedia*. Supplementary material includes maps, charts, and illustrations. A special supplement to the commentary, volume 7-A, contains pertinent Ellen G. White comments.

Volume 1, Genesis to Deuteronomy, US$35.95, Cdn$44.95.

Volume 2, Joshua to 2 Kings, US$35.95, Cdn$44.95.

Volume 3, 1 Chronicles to Song of Solomon, US$35.95, Cdn$44.95.

Volume 4, Isaiah to Malachi, US$35.95, Cdn$44.95.

Volume 5, Matthew to John, US$35.95, Cdn$44.95.

Volume 6, Acts to Ephesians, US$35.95, Cdn$44.95.

Volume 7, Philippians to Revelation, US$35.95, Cdn$44.95.

Volume 7-A, Ellen G. White Comments, US$18.95, Cdn$23.70.

Volume 8, SDA Bible Dictionary, US$35.95, Cdn$44.95.

Volume 9, SDA Bible Students' Source Book, US$35.95, Cdn$44.95.

Volume 10, SDA Encyclopedia, US$35.95, Cdn$44.95.

Complete commentary set (volume 7-A not included), US$329.50, Cdn$411.90.

Call or write your Adventist Book Center to order, or write to: ABC Mailing Service, P.O. Box 1119, Hagerstown, MD 21741. Send check or money order. Enclose applicable sales tax and 15 percent (minimum US$2.50) for postage and handling. Prices and availability subject to change without notice.

Call Your ABC Toll-free
1-800-765-6955